BIRMINGHAM VOL I

Edited by Donna Samworth

First published in Great Britain in 2003 by
YOUNG WRITERS
Remus House,
Coltsfoot Drive,
Peterborough, PE2 9JX
Telephone (01733) 890066

HB ISBN 0 75434 215 8
SB ISBN 0 75434 216 6

Foreword

This year, the Young Writers' The Write Stuff! competition proudly presents a showcase of the best poetic talent from over 40,000 up-and-coming writers nationwide.

Young Writers was established in 1991 and we are still successful, even in today's modern world, in promoting and encouraging the reading and writing of poetry.

The thought, effort, imagination and hard work put into each poem impressed us all, and once again, the task of selecting poems was a difficult one, but nevertheless, an enjoyable experience.

We hope you are as pleased as we are with the final selection and that you and your family continue to be entertained with *The Write Stuff! Birmingham Vol I* for many years to come.

CONTENTS

The Poems

For What Is Love?

A lone bird soars,
Soars into the deep blue sky,
So calm, so innocent
Its wings softly beating the air it flies,
Flies into the distance,
So far, so gentle.

A sudden gunfire breaks the tranquil scene,
The sky turns black with smoke,
So dark, so bleak.
There is screaming as the guns fire,
Much screaming,
So loud, so sad.

The women and children flee,
The men remain to fight,
So scared, so brave.

The rain pours down,
Down on the defending heroes,
So bleak, so endless

There is death,
Death everywhere,
So cruel, so destructive

But the battle rages on,
They are too proud to end it,
So stubborn, so blind

There is no love,
For what is love?
Love is pure and bright, it is everything

The men are brave,
but in years to come,
they will be forgotten.

Nicola Caton (12)
Edgbaston High School For Girls

I'm Woken Up In The Morning By Something Very Strange . . .

I'm woken up in the morning by something very strange,
Men wearing dresses,
With lipstick on their faces.

I'm woken up in the morning by something very strange,
Ladies wearing ties,
While surrounded by smelly flies.

I'm woken up in the morning by something very strange,
The animals are talking
And everybody's crawling.

I'm woken up in the morning by something very strange,
My cat is walking upside down,
My fish looks like it's going to drown.

I wake up in the morning,
To find it's all a dream,
I just think I had too much of Gran's cauliflower supreme!

Saffia Ahmed (12)
Edgbaston High School For Girls

Winter

W alking out the door is like walking into a thousand ice cubes.
I ce skating is a favourite sport this time of year.
N ourishing cups of tea are a saviour when you come in
out of the cold.
T he clocks go back like going to New York.
E laborate decorations are put up for Christmas.
R aincoats are worn like T-shirts in summer.

Lily Tomkins (11)
Edgbaston High School For Girls

TYPICAL TEENAGE MORNING

You wake up in the morning,
Half an hour late
And think to yourself,
My god, what a state.

Last night's mascara,
Smudged down your face.
Think to yourself,
What a disgrace!

Then there's the hair,
Where on earth is the brush?
Oh you haven't got time,
You're in such a rush.

Up it goes,
In that scruffy bun.
I'm tellin' you now,
This certainly ain't fun!

'Come on!' yells Mum,
'You'll be late for school.'
Flippin' heck,
You don't half look a fool.

Well I suppose it's a start,
You're out of bed.
But with breath like that,
You'll wake the dead!

You make it to school,
Not paying attention
And you get yourself
A week of detention!

Kelsey Moyce (12)
Edgbaston High School For Girls

NATURE'S BEAUTY

I lie here alone with the grass in my hair,
In a field I throw my arms to the air.
Time floats past,
Slower than the hourglass,
The quietness laughs with noise
As I appreciate Nature's toys.
The way the birds sing and the horses play,
The way I feel so safe as each hour is a day.
The air moves over me,
As Mother Nature breathes
Caressing her land and swaying her trees.
Times does not stop, only slows down,
As I feel myself leave the ground,
Running away, the wind in my hair,
Freedom engulfs me as I stop to stare.
I stand there alone,
Not a care in the world
And for just one second I know true joy,
As my heart is lifted, I smile unknowingly
As I see the picture standing before me.
Nature plays her song of wind and water
And all I can do is lie down in the grass
And appreciate it all at last.

Rachel Shipley (13)
Edgbaston High School For Girls

LOVE

Love is like an angel in disguise
Love is like a dove in the sky
Love is like a wolf in search of its prey
Love is like a child at play.

Love can be beautiful
Love can be sweet
Love can be painful
And love can be deep.

Karen Buchanan (12)
Edgbaston High School For Girls

Look At Me

Look at me,
What do you see?
Everything I'm meant to be?
No.

Perfect hair?
Perfect eyes?
Perfect clothes?
No.

Good at gym?
Good at maths?
Good at physics?
No.

Another face?
Another side?
Another person?
Yes.

Now look at me,
What do you see?
Everything I'm meant to be?
You decide.

Emily Pittaway (12)
Edgbaston High School For Girls

Falling Off The Tips Of My Fingers

Me as in me.
Friend as in friend.
Best friend as in best friend.
Close friend as in close friend.

Me and my best friend.
Close as can be.
Going through tough times,
With her comforting me.

One day I walked into school,
To talk to my best friend.
Only to find that my best friend
No longer found me cool.

My best friend going off with my friend,
Saying things about me,
Whilst me and my close friend
Spoke quietly together in our den.

Days went by,
While me and my close friend
Began to realise that our friendship
Was strengthening and growing very high.

I think me and my close friend
Are best friends.
And my best friend is just my friend,
While she's falling off the tips of my fingers.

Sharnaz Shahid (12)
Edgbaston High School For Girls

THE LIFE OF A SHOE

I am a brand new shoe in a shop,
Sitting on a shelf,
Waiting to be worn,
Waiting to have an owner.

After hours of sitting and waiting,
My buyer finally comes along,
Her face lights up when she sees me,
I've finally found a home.

I get wrapped up in a cardboard box,
I can feel myself being lifted up,
My other shoe companion is with me,
Where are we going? I hope we have a nice owner.

We are taken out of the cardboard box,
She picks me up,
I feel her foot move around inside me,
Then she slams me down on the floor.

My owner takes her first step outside in us,
There is a crunch underneath,
She has trodden in dirt and leaves,
We are filthy already.

I will never look brand new again,
But I will look old and scruffy,
I preferred sitting on the shelf all day,
But now, it's too late.

Jennie Allen (13)
Edgbaston High School For Girls

WINTER

Cold icy fingers reach out.
Coldness sweeps past you, leaving you frozen.
Jack Frost jumps out; all becomes white, icy blue,
Feet crunch
Freezing fingertips.
Snow like a white blanket covering green.
Leaves coated in a layer of clear ice.
Ice on the pavement glistening.
Icicles like deformed crystals,
The smell of Christmas wafting past your nose,
Warm mince pies,
Snowflakes melting on your hand.
Jack Frost's cold wind overcomes you,
Suddenly you see a ray of sunshine,
Snow starts melting,
The last snowflake falls.
The first flower blossoms.

Sophie Brookes (11)
Edgbaston High School For Girls

MY MACAW

You should see my macaw
She's broken every single law.

She loves her food cooked or raw
Even pieces of apple core!

I was told about her by a man using a saw,
So I bought her from the pet store.

She's always perching upon the door
Peering out across the moor.

Isabel Gaskell (11)
Edgbaston High School For Girls

WINTER

Skies are duller
Winter's come again
Skies are like sugar shakers
Sprinkling snow around.

It's Christmas time
Children are playing in flaky snow
Hot Christmas dinners
Decorated Christmas trees.

Foggy cold mornings!
Build up blazing fires
Better hang up my stocking
Santa's coming soon.

Better wrap up warm
Hats, coats, gloves, scarves
My feet feel like icicles
My fingers feel like ice!

Abigail Wright (12)
Edgbaston High School For Girls

WINTER

It was muggy; rather cold on that grey morning,
My feet were freezing, icicles drooped from windows,
Everything was white with glistening snow,
Falling all around were tiny snowflakes,
Footprints of small animals feet in deep, crispy snow,
Snow lay around everything, the plants were crystallised,
I was entering a sparkling world.

Hannah Davis (11)
Edgbaston High School For Girls

PLEASE MR PROCTOR

(Based on 'Please Mrs Butler' by Allan Ahlberg)

Please Mr Proctor,
This girl Lucy Loo,
She keeps taking my pencil, Sir,
What shall I do?

Keep writing with it, my dear,
Put it in your bag,
Hide it from her, my girl,
Do whatever you can.

Please Mr Proctor,
This girl Lucy Loo,
She keeps staring at me, Sir,
What shall I do?

Use your common sense girl,
Go and sit somewhere else,
Keep your eyes down
And look at something different.

Please Mr Proctor,
This girl Lucy Loo,
She keeps singing, Sir,
What shall I do?

Put something in your ears, dear,
Fingers will do,
Sort out your own problems
And stop annoying me!

Charlotte Buckle (11)
Edgbaston High School For Girls

THE PIANO

The piano was old and dusty,
With faded ivory keys
All seeming to cry out for a tune,
Someone to play and enjoy
Its old and dusty keys.

It had been in the attic for years,
Ever since they'd bought the new one
And heartlessly replaced it,
After all those years of faithful service
With an ebony grand piano.

Never again will it see the light of day,
Just sits in the attic,
The imprint of a thousand melodies upon its keys
With just its beautiful, vivid memories to keep it company
And connect it with the luxurious life it once had.

It wishes it could speak or sing,
To tell its story to the world
Of concerts and balls, recitals and feasts,
Before it forgets
Or is forgotten.

It is not fair,
That this regal instrument
That still plays sharp and true,
Should be shut up in a tiny space
And allowed to slip from all memory.

Caroline Halstead Smith (13)
Edgbaston High School For Girls

WINTER

Delicate snowflakes falling,
Snowmen built by tiny cold hands.
Warm fires glowing.
December 25th,
Everyone's happy!
Snow-covered treetops.
Animals hibernating,
Blood-ridden faces,
Colds and flu.
Deadly roads.
Jack Frost's icy fingers,
The Snow Queen's magic wand.
Lovely Christmas puddings.
Woolly hats,
Woolly scarves,
Woolly socks,
Woolly gloves and coats.
Winter.

Radha Soni (11)
Edgbaston High School For Girls

COLONEL FAZACKERLY

As Colonel Fazackerly got into bed
He heard strange noises in his head
Of laughter, clanging and banging too!
Oh who was doing this, oh who?

It's turning itself inside out
Hoping that you will shout
It takes off its toes and also its nose
And it makes himself turn into a rose.

Charlotte Utton (11)
Edgbaston High School For Girls

WINTER

Wrap up warm, winter is here,
Round the corner is the new year.
I wonder whether they'll be some snow
Maybe some ice, I don't know.

Sometimes it's cold and your nose goes red,
But it's much nicer to stay in bed.
Drinking soup and eating meat,
In front of the fire with all the heat.

Out in the cold, the animals hide
And on the ice, the old folk slide.
Splashing in puddles made by the rain,
Sometimes it's fun, sometimes it's a pain.

Out pops the winter sun,
Warming the land, thaw has begun.
February passes, birds start to sing,
A sign that winter has passed . . .
And here comes spring!

Eman Messahel (11)
Edgbaston High School For Girls

WINTER

W ithering willows curl up -
Even the oldest and strongest have been taken in by its power.
I ntertwining snowdrops fall against the windows.
N umb fingers retire from making snowmen.
T he bragging bully, the wind, bites at people's toes.
E ver falling snow like a salt shaker.
R ain is no more, the hard, harsh hailstones take over.
We have been beaten by *winter.*

Sarah Learmonth (12)
Edgbaston High School For Girls

POEMS

Some poems are good
Some poems are great
Some poems I love
Some poems I hate

Some poems are serious
Some poems are funny
Some poems are sold
So poets make money!

Some poems are stories
Some poems are limericks
Some poems are sonnets
Some poems are silly

Some poems rhyme
Some poems don't
No poems say 'purple'
'Cause it doesn't rhyme!

Ruth Beattie (12)
Edgbaston High School For Girls

WINTER

W ind blowing against my ice-cold cheeks
I cicles hanging off trees
N umb fingers and toes
I can't feel my nose
T hawing in front of the fire is all that I desire
E very step I take feels like a thousand miles!
Don't think I can take it . . .
R eaching home at last,
I can make it.

Riman Khangure (11)
Edgbaston High School For Girls

FIELDS

Fields long,
Fields wide,
All in the countryside.

Full of sheep,
Full of cows,
Full of farmers
With their ploughs.

Corn, wheat,
Barley, maize,
Each one for
Different days.

Tractors and horses
With bundles of hay,
To put in the chicken coop,
For the hens to lay.

Fields long,
Fields wide,
All in the countryside.

Joanna Keen (12)
Edgbaston High School For Girls

HORSES

H orses eat a lot of hay
Br O wn, chestnut, grey and bay
R acing round the field they go
S ome fast and some slow
E very day they start to neigh
S o there they go, cantering away.

Ayesha Banks (13)
Edgbaston High School For Girls

Winter

Snow falling like drips of water,
Snowdrops looking like pure pearls,
Snowflakes making shapes of spider webs,
Ice being formed on smooth grounds,
Whilst flakes fall, children make snowmen,
Frost begins to build up on windows,
Fires inside houses turn on,
Children start snowball fights,
Hands chill like ice,
Adults snuggle up in cosy blankets,
Bright coloured lights glow everywhere outside,
Suddenly snowdrops melt,
Winter had gone!

Vishika Patel (11)
Edgbaston High School For Girls

Holiday Time

Hustling like a shopper in the sales,
Bustling in the bulging bathroom,
Scurrying like a hurrying mouse,
Alarm clock resounding in the crisp, chill dawn.
'Where's the note for the milkman?'
'Is the cat next door?'
Stampeding elephants trampling down the stairs,
A bowl of cereal with forgotten milk,
Trekking to the car with a tonne of cases,
Still munching toast like lions half-starved,
A hiccup of engines and a jolt of metal.
'Goodbye.'

Stephanie Edwards (13)
Edgbaston High School For Girls

Pandora

It took the shape of a woman,
Deathly thin,
Long and tall,
Her eyes robbed of their shine,
Her skin a pale, waxy white,
Her lips two rolls of salmon-pink flesh,
With a head of scraggy, thin strands of hair
And arms and legs like long, slender sticks,
With flimsy droops of flesh hanging from them,
She had once been beautiful,
But hunger had sucked her dry to the bone
And sickness swarmed over her,
Until she had been banished to this world of pain,
Who would have known the evil she had unleashed,
To a world so innocent,
Just by opening a box.

Christina Hawker (13)
Edgbaston High School For Girls

My School

Edgbaston High is my school,
my favourite lesson is in the pool.
I'm happy here with all my friends,
we try to keep up with the latest trends.

There is so much homework which gets me down
and when my mum sees it, it makes her frown.
She tries to help but it goes over her head,
so I have to ask my brother instead.

Apart from that I like it here
and hope I have a very good year.

Charlotte Woodroffe (11)
Edgbaston High School For Girls

1984

Burning sun
Beating down on marble slabs.
Too hot for bare feet.
The sun shining off the gold
Into their eyes
And making brown faces
Even browner.

Tanks approaching
Soldiers marching
Entrances blocked.
Yet inside the golden shelter
The prayer goes on.
Under order, the men of the country
Close their eyes and shoot.

Memories of half a century ago
Rush through people's minds.
A woman forever sleeping
Someone's mother, someone's sister, someone's daughter.
Bullets rip through the air
Piercing, harming and killing
Even the precious water holds no safety.

The gunfire stops
But the pain is everlasting.
Children cry for their mothers
Men cry for their families.
A shirt dyed red
Getting redder
And the prayer has stopped.

History always repeats itself.

Tej Kaur Rai (15)
Edgbaston High School For Girls

Why?

Hyesha?
Yes . . .
Why are you wearing that?
I'm wearing it because it's my school uniform.
But why?
Because I have to wear it to go to school.
Why?
So people know what school I go to.
Why?
Because I do!
Hyesha?
Yes!
What's school?
A place where you learn things.
Why?
To get a good job when you're older.
Why?
To earn good money!
Hyesha?
Yes!
Why do you learn?
Because you do!
Why?
I told you why!
Why?
Stop saying why!
Why?
Just stop it right now!
Why?
Because *you're annoying me, that's why!*
Why?
Urgh!

Hyesha Rahanu (14)
Edgbaston High School For Girls

Watching Out The Window

Watching out the window
Letting the world go by
Seeing people laugh
Seeing people cry.

Watching out the window
Letting the world go by
People having rages
In many different ages.

Watching out the window
Letting the world go by
People queuing for buses
Mothers making fusses.

Watching out the window
Letting the world go by
Lights flash
People dash.

Elizabeth Verow (12)
Edgbaston High School For Girls

Autumn At 1am

His feet rustle
And my neck is held
In winter's noose
Thoughts may slumber
Cold and envious
But people wonder
Their faces tight
With passing sadness
As I walk out into the road.

Alice Naylor (16)
Edgbaston High School For Girls

The Trolley

I work for a firm called Waitrose.
I am stacked in lots of long rows.
I long to be brand new once more.
I was pushed into a river last week, along with a door.
I hate my job, I get battered and wrecked.
My lustrous metal frame starts to rust when wet.

When I am pushed down the aisle
I start to smile, I know I will take the stresses and strains.
I get so worn out my wheels start to ache.
I am glad when we get to the checkout,
As I am relieved of my weight.

No one has any respect for me and my friends.
We're the ones who meet your needs in the end.
So when you next care your shopping to do,
Remember I have feelings just like you.

Rachael Collard (13)
Edgbaston High School For Girls

Danae's Love For Zeus

Danae's love for Zeus was incredibly overwhelming.
She was immediately captured by his beauty,
She stared adoringly into his golden brown eyes,
But when she found out he didn't feel the same way
She stared forlornly into the far distance,
The irritation inside was so strong,
She knew the gods could hear her pain,
With this she chanted to the heavens,
'Let Zeus feel the same distress as I.'

Charlotte Jones-Cope (12)
Edgbaston High School For Girls

The Radiator

I am a radiator,
stuffed in the back of B&Q,
on a dusty display.

Wiped by a wet, cold wipe,
all dust removed from my belly,
cold hands touched me and hauled me around,
towards a red car.

Placed on a warm, furry surface,
where I was very comfortable,
then awoken as we turned sharp corners.

The cold hands touched me again
and carried me into a warm, snug home.
My skin was rapidly ripped off,
I felt cold and bare, held against a yellow wall.

Now screwed on, hanging bare on the wall,
I get turned on and off, hot and cold.

Harriet Barnett (13)
Edgbaston High School For Girls

Winter

Frosty, chilly mornings,
That whip you round your face,
Little pink noses,
Fingers like blocks of ice.

Children playing in snow,
Wrapped up warm in cosy clothes,
To prevent that evil man,
From coming to make them shiver.

Christmas is so very near,
Families prepare for an exciting time,
Going out,
Having fun too,
Festive cheer is so enjoyable.

Christina Tavener (11)
Edgbaston High School For Girls

THE CHRISTMAS FAIRY

I'm the Christmas fairy,
Sitting on top of the tree,
Happy I am as people go by,
Admiring my wings with glee.

Many people admire the tree,
With green leaves, ugly, compared to me,
People forget to look at me,
As I am sitting on top of the tree.

Happy children come and go,
But I am here all year round,
Standing on a box in a shop window here,
I look out over the road which is near.

A little girl is looking in
And asking her mummy if she can go in,
She walks inside and looks at me,
Her little face is full of glee.

She takes me to the till,
He gives the girl her bill,
She gives the man the money,
Now I'm feeling a bit ill . . .

Emma Matts (13)
Edgbaston High School For Girls

The Pencil Case

Here I am on a shelf,
All empty and alone,
Waiting for that moment when
Someone will take me home.

My many pretty colours
Would brighten any face.
With my pink and purple stitching
And a blue and turquoise base.

My outside layer is soft,
Fluffy like a cloud,
My inside layer is velvet,
With colours bright and loud.

I dream of carrying stationery,
Pencils, rubber, pen,
I know it in my furry heart
That day will come, but when?

I look at the 'Quiksilver' tin,
And I am jealous to see,
That all the children are buying him
And none are buying me.

All the girls and boys
Stopped to look and stare,
At the 'Quiksilver' pencil case,
But I don't really care.

At last some interest,
Yes in me,
From the depth of her bag,
A purse I do see!

She picks me up, moves to the till,
Oh my goodness, she's paid the bill!

Katie Coe (14)
Edgbaston High School For Girls

Brain-Dead

I cannot take in anymore,
My head is getting very sore.
Teachers, teachers keep on talking,
All I do is keep on working.
I wonder where it will all end,
I need to chat to my best friend.

Tomorrow is another day,
We really do need time to play,
Happy play in grassy places
Perhaps some time to tie my laces.

Our teachers need us all to learn,
Our welfare is their main concern,
Our parents want us to achieve
But give our brains a chance to breathe.

We've only just left junior school,
We never want to look like fools,
We're trying hard to do our best
But sometimes brain cells need a rest.

Diamond Lee-Harris (11)
Edgbaston High School For Girls

The Belfry Tower

The traveller climbed the belfry tower,
His eyes were hollows of madness,
His feet made no sound on the belfry tower
And he burned and seethed for poor Agnes.

When the world was young and full of life,
He'd courted her in the blue cornflower,
They were young, spirited, full of life,
Lost from now on the belfry tower.

That summer filled the dale with song,
Which sleeps in the earth when it no longer sounds,
It now sings in the breeze, a melancholy strain,
Sung by a waif who was lost and not found.

Lost in the sea from that cursed belfry tower,
The traveller glared at the waves,
She sang, enticing, from the blue cornflower,
In his madness, he was her slave.

In that last fleeting moment, he hammered a curse,
Of pain, anger, despair,
Then, his earthly existence had come to an end,
Once again, silence reigned there.

And they say, in the summer when lovers walk,
And the wind whispers softly in the blue cornflower,
That the traveller and Agnes sing with the wind,
Far from the monolithic belfry tower.

Cydney Johnson (13)
Edgbaston High School For Girls

The Death Of A Relative

A man awaited his end;
Thoughts racing through his brain.
'Will anyone hear me?' he cried,
The dying man moaning.

He was a great man in his pride,
Leading others who stood by his side.
Now it was time to be put to rest,
Where he would live in peace and harmony.

He began to wonder what would happen to him,
Wherever he was going.
Would he be watching down on us?
Wishing he'd lived his life as we were living ours?

As he lay on the deathbed,
I knew what he wanted to say;
This man with all the pride in the world,
Wanted to open a door into his heart and pray.

He left many folk devastated,
When his time on Earth was done.
Yet, still I know he will always be there,
Waiting patiently to help and guide me through life.

If I died this very day
And I had one last wish to fulfil,
I'd ask to spend it with him
And we'd relive our childhood dreams.

Natasha Ilsley (13)
Edgbaston High School For Girls

The Carpet In The Hall

Last month I got cleaned,
That was when I was new,
A table was put on my belly,
A chair on my shoe.

My owners have four children,
Sweets land heavily on my skin.
When Susie goes out
Her heels dig right in.

Dinner parties are the worst,
Wine, beer, chocolate,
All over me,
They don't finish till late.

When Kevin goes gardening,
When Peter goes to play football,
Dirty wellies, muddy boots,
On me, the carpet in the hall.

Helen Aldred (13)
Edgbaston High School For Girls

My Baby Brother

I love my baby brother
he is only 3 months
but sometimes I wish
he would just shut up.

I love my baby brother
he is so, so sweet
but sometimes I think
he could be quite mean.

I love my baby brother
he always likes to play
I love the way he is
and I hope he will stay this way.

Anisah Shoaib (12)
Edgbaston High School For Girls

THE TOOTH FAIRY

I am a little fairy,
all sparkly and white,
I like to shine brightly during the night.
I go and collect the teeth
and take them home,
so I place them in my basket
and skip back to my home in Rome.

I get out the teeth that I have collected
and start to clean them as expected,
look at them now,
all shiny and new,
I'm still not sure what I should do
shall I keep them as nice gifts
or give them away to the people I miss?

It's getting very dark now
it's time for me to sleep
I'll put on my nightgown,
all fluffy and pink,
I'll turn out the lights
until the morning is due,
so goodnight from me now
and goodnight to you.

Rebecca Roe (13)
Edgbaston High School For Girls

FOOTPRINTS ON THE SAND

My memories of you,
Are like footprints on the sand,
Dreaming of the old days,
When we walked hand in hand.

Trying to forget you,
Is like nailing jelly to a tree
And I sometimes wish the old days,
Would come back to me.

The ocean takes the footprints
And carries them off the shore,
But in my mind they'll always stay,
They are here for evermore.

I dream of those fragile footprints,
I won't let be washed away,
They are printed on my heart,
Where they will always stay.

And to try to save them,
The memories are inside my hand,
To protect them from the waves of time,
Like footprints on the sand.

Laura Caton (13)
Edgbaston High School For Girls

UNTITLED

Tonight I wait, wait for the dark shrouded figure
with the bayonet, I see him at the end of every day,
he collects the men who have fallen.
He cuts their ties to earthly matters
and lets them go with honour.

Then he comes to the trenches, searching,
wait . . . wait, there! A flurry of movement.
A slow exhalation of breath,
the transition from living creature to cooling meat.
He turns, waves and points at me.
I know it will be my turn next . . .
After tomorrow I shan't see him again.

Elizabeth Stone (14)
Edgbaston High School For Girls

THE STARS ARE LIKE . . .

The stars are like tiny ducklings,
Swimming in the sparkling lake,
The stars are like weird-shaped cookies,
Which I am just about to bake,
The stars are like little daisies,
Flying in the dark blue sky,
The stars are like shining diamonds,
Which I would love to buy.

Laura Chung (11)
Edgbaston High School For Girls

WINTER

W ind like a howling wolf.
I ncredible snow like a polar bear's skin.
N ight skies are black as coal.
T he rain like millions of sapphires falling from the sky.
E xtreme cold so severe it's like it's biting your face,
R eindeers galloping like stars in the sky.

Josie Smith (11)
Edgbaston High School For Girls

Life Was Never Meant To Be Easy

Grown-ups think that just because I'm young I never understand,
They think I daydream and bury my head in the sand

. . . But they don't imagine what I think and what I know
When I have my high points and when I have my low.

Why don't people tell me things instead of locking them away?
Explaining fears and matters each and every day.

Life was never meant to be easy,
With people being unkind and sleazy.

Everything is possible so never ever give in
And you can face every challenge even with a grin.

Annie Metcalfe (12)
Edgbaston High School For Girls

The Mirror

Standing on the landing I am clean, modern and sleek.
I tower over the rug, which looks like a rubbish heap.

Standing on the landing, I am looked at every day.
Unlike the lamp whose only use is to light up people's way.

Standing on the landing, I show people things they don't want to see.
That's why the terribly dressed rush past me.

Standing on the landing, I await my prey.
'Oh dear, I look awful,' they all seem to say.

Standing on the landing, I suddenly crack.
When someone fed up with my total honesty, stabs me in the back.

Helen Jennison (13)
Edgbaston High School For Girls

Far From Home

As you see the sea swaying to and fro,
It makes you think how far, far away you are from home.
You're thinking about your family
And wondering if they ever think of you.
So you decide to ring them,
Before it gets too late
And thinking what you're going to say too.
You ring and ring till someone answers,
Then they finally do.
Your mum asks how you are
And tells you that you're not too far.
She says to you when you are homesick
To look inside your heart
And remember that they will always be there
Just where you are!

Sunam Mukhtar (12)
Edgbaston High School For Girls

The Phone

The phone is an amazing thing
It often goes *ring, ring.*
The bill can fill three pages
And cost me all my wages.

I can spend hours on the phone
Listening to friends moan,
I'm trying to think who rang who
As it is me who made the call,
I can definitely forget
That bouncy ball!

Lois Hamilton (12)
Edgbaston High School For Girls

THE GIRL

The girl sits alone,
In a cold eerie graveyard.
The leaves rustle on the floor,
As her mind races.

She thinks about a friendship,
One she used to treasure.
Now there's just an empty space,
The pieces have slipped through her fingers.

It is long gone now,
She has been thrown into turmoil.
The memories are still there though,
Her enemy, making her remember.
She feels confused and lost.

Everyone turns her away,
The 'cool' group and the 'brainy' ones.
She listens to the taunts and sarcasm.
How could her old friend be so cold?
She searches for the answer.

Her friend keeps using her though,
As a person to fall back on.
She falls for it every time too,
Laying herself open to more hurt.

A pained look across her face,
She takes a deep breath.
Her last breath.

Laura Millership (13)
Edgbaston High School For Girls

The Bin

Here I sit in the theme park,
Next to my best friend Rory,
We have had many fun times together,
Sometimes with his brother Mark.

Many people say hello to me,
Many just walk on by,
Many don't even notice me,
Some are moving so fast they flee.

People feed me trash.
Apple cores and meat,
Some give me proper food,
Sausage, peas and mash.

I wait endlessly, ready to be fed,
Although it never works,
Rory normally does better than me,
So sometimes I just go to bed.

When I am full, I am emptied,
When I am broken, I am dull,
When I am sad, I am made better,
When I am hungry, I am not glad.

My life is about to end now,
As I have been thrashed and kicked around,
I suppose I will be moved to a dumping ground,
I will really miss my pals.

Emma Baxter (13)
Edgbaston High School For Girls

THE CHRISTMAS BAUBLE

It's nearly time to get out of this box.
A box full of baubles weighed down with locks,
It is very dark and scary.
Colours and shapes of us do vary.

At last today is the day,
When we all come out to play,
We are hung upon the Christmas tree
Left to hang on the branch free.

Now festivity is all around
The bells at the church make a lovely sound
Christmas is now officially here,
My favourite time of year.

Kelly Barnes (13)
Edgbaston High School For Girls

THE MOON

On a dark and windy night
The sparkling moon shines silver bright
Helping people find their way
To their homes at the end of the day.

Its rays meet a shooting star
That has travelled from afar
As it drops beneath the world
The sun starts to unfurl.

Once again all is bright
Filled by the sun's eternal light
The sphere shines glittery gold
Illuminating the entire world.

Olivia Hemsoll (13)
Edgbaston High School For Girls

Smoochykins - The Kitten

There was a little kitty called Smoochykins,
who was pretty as could be.
She was owned by a little girl called Rosy.
Rosy was thought to be an adorable child
but actually quite a devil was she.
She loved her lovely Smoochy so much
she dressed her all in pink!
One day little Smoochy - dressed in pink -
into the garden went she.
While having her little walk
she met a big wolf standing on the grass.
This wolf ate dear Smoochy up for his tea.
When poor Rosy came out to play
all that was left was her pink bows and tail.

Joanna Millward (11)
Edgbaston High School For Girls

I'm Sure My Brother Is A Vampire!

I'm sure my brother is a vampire
I really know it's true
He never eats his garlic bread
He stuffs it in his shoe
He's never in family photos
Because of the flashing light!
He's never ever liked me
And always wants to bite me!
He never ever goes to church
And always stays at home.
I wonder what he does,
When he's all alone?

Sophie Cooper (12)
Edgbaston High School For Girls

SOAP

I arrive in a shopping bag,
All brand new,
Wrapped up in a cardboard box,
Waiting eagerly to be opened by my owner.

The box is opened up,
I see her face so pale and wrinkly,
Is this the right owner?
I ask myself.

She puts me on the side of her bath,
It's green with mould growing on the side,
My new home,
I preferred the shelf.

A few days later she gets in the bath,
And reaches for me,
She rubs me on her wrinkly body,
I wonder, can I be sick?

As the weeks pass I deteriorate,
Slowly losing my touch,
I don't foam anymore,
Or make her as clean as much as I did.

Then one day, one summer's day,
She buys a new soap,
I'm picked up and disposed of in the bin
With the packaging of my enemy.

The end has come,
You'll never hear from me again,
I'm going to a better place
The tip.

Kam Atwal (13)
Edgbaston High School For Girls

MONDAY, THERE'S A TRAFFIC JAM . . .

Monday	There's a traffic jam all the way to school
and you're yawning and you're miserable
and feeling such a fool.

Tuesday	Lessons aren't too bad, there's lots of different clubs.
Teacher's in a better mood and things are looking up.

Wednesday	Is in the middle, not the beginning, not the end
They're piling on the homework,
It drives me round the bend.

Thursday's	Great, PE and art,
Music, drama and maths, if you're smart.

Friday	Clocks are not your friend,
Bells ring late and there's a rush at the end.

Saturday	Dawn's, there's, a lie-in for some
But not if you're sporty, the netball's begun.

Sunday	Should be heavenly but there's homework left to do
So little time to finish it and now I'm feeling blue.

Monday	There's a traffic jam . . .

Sarah Baker (11)
Edgbaston High School For Girls

SPRING

S pring is like the end of school bell on a Friday afternoon.
P rancing lambs like little frogs.
R ed flowers pop up like little bunnies.
I ndigo is like rich velvet cloaks.
N ights are shorter like sand running through an egg timer.
G ilded stars frame with icy sky like black velvet.

Lillie Gregg (11)
Edgbaston High School For Girls

ALONE

I'm all alone, nothing to say, nothing to do.
Do is something I can only do when I'm not alone,
Alone, walking around, there's no place to roam,
Roam about endlessly, I wish I had a home.

Home, I will still be alone, it makes me cry, makes me weak,
Weak is something I'm becoming, sooner, sooner,
Sooner or later I will stop trying,
Trying is something so hard, I don't want to give up on.

On the days when I am happy,
Happiness will soon go,
Go round alone, night and day,
Day makes me sad, just another day alone.

Alone is something I will always be,
Be something that's not me, that's not right,
Right, left, there is nowhere to turn,
Turn around, there's no friend, no home.

Home I will never have if I am all alone,
Alone, always I've got to get away from here,
Here I will stay, until it is time,
Time for me to lay back and die.

Kyriaki Koumi (12)
Edgbaston High School For Girls

I WISH, I WISH

I wish I was a cat
Lazing around all day,
I wish I was a dog
Going for walks and to play,
I wish I was a fish
Swimming in the deep blue sea,
I wish I was anything, anyone but boring me.

I wish I was a bird up in the sky,
Wouldn't it be wonderful, flying so high?
I wish I was an eagle soaring through the air,
Wouldn't it be wonderful to live without a care?
I wish I was a seagull
Living by the sea,
I wish I was anything, anyone but boring me!

Jenny Owen (14)
Edgbaston High School For Girls

SUMMER

Shimmering sun
Bronzed beaches
Crystal clear seas
Seagulls circling overhead
The scavengers search for scraps

Colourful carnivals clash

Soothing waves
Lap over sandy shores
Seas of happy faces
Volleyball nets
Cooling currents flow

The beautiful briny sea

Rocks rise like stepping stones
Which hang over turquoise waters
End of summer brings mourning faces

The summer sheds its skin
They leave summer with joyful memories
That shall not be forgotten.

Sarah Thind (11)
Edgbaston High School For Girls

VISITING THE DENTIST

I go into the waiting room
and sat upon a chair,
waiting for them to call my name
when I saw someone standing there.

They then called out a name,
but luckily it wasn't me.
I knew that I would be next though,
so my head buried in my knee.

My name was then read out,
I stood up feeling blue.
I walked up to the dreaded room,
and there was Doctor Who.

He stood there with the needles
and gave me an evil stare.
I stood as still as ice,
as he called me towards the chair.

This is when I began to shake
as I looked towards the light.
He rapidly came towards my mouth,
which gave me quite a fright.

All that I remember is
that I woke up with a start.
What was all the fuss about,
the racing of my heart.

Coralie McCutcheon (13)
Edgbaston High School For Girls

My New School

My new school is far away,
Not close and safe to home.
What shall I do when I get there?
Will I be all alone?

Will I like my teacher?
Will she be young or old?
I'll try to be good and please her
Will she say I'm as good as gold?

I'll travel to school on a bus
That collects me from my door,
It's calling early to fetch me
I'll stay up late no more.

I'll have to make some friends
To make the days go well,
I'll choose them very carefully
I'll like it I can tell.

The day has come to go to school
The bus came right on time,
The school is big with lots of girls
My teacher - she'll do fine.

I'm feeling very safe now
I seem to know the rules,
There's lots to do and lots to learn
It's the best of all the schools.

Charlotte Cheetham (11)
Edgbaston High School For Girls

MY SPACE

In my bedroom I have got
Cushions, teddies, an awful lot
Of junk that I have never used
And most of it has been abused.

The fact that my bedroom is a tip,
Is down to my brother's little trip
To my bedroom every night
That normally ends up in a fight.

When I tell my mum and dad
That my brother has been very bad
They go and give him a big smack
But that doesn't stop him from coming back.

My friends are welcome in my pad
But not my brother, his mates or my dad.
My mum, well that really is another matter
She comes to have a little natter.

They take no notice
Of the sign *Beware!*
Perhaps they will
When they get a scare.

Natalie Griffiths (11)
Edgbaston High School For Girls

SPEAK OUT!

Sometimes I am fed up and shout
But when you are in trouble you do not speak out.
Unless I insist but you always resist,
Perhaps you do not trust me,
Or don't have courage maybe.

Please do not curse me and yourself
Encourage yourself and speak out.
Share with me your grief and sorrow
Trust me today and tomorrow
And always and always.

Fatima Shah (12)
Edgbaston High School For Girls

Counting The Seconds

Time seems to go so slowly
Time seems to go so fast
It ticks away day after day
How long will time last?

Time won't always be there
It will slip away like sand
I wish that I could keep it
In the palm of my hand

However fast you can run
Time can run much faster
There's no point trying to beat the clock
As time is your harsh master

Time is running out
I keep glancing at the clock
There is still one question left to answer
What happens when time stops?

Your time on Earth is finite
Waste your time and you'll be sad
A fitting epitaph would be
'I did it' not 'I wish I had'.

Laura Warton (12)
Edgbaston High School For Girls

The Field Of War

In the field of war love is great,
Love for country not for a friend,
You must be strong in the field of war,
People may die, but their death is in vain.
No difference did they make I thought,
But they did, as without one man
An army is incomplete,
It is like the saying, 'Every penny counts.'

In the field of war the atmosphere is poor,
But the courage of each individual was excessive.
Life goes on if your friend desists his life.
Life left behind still goes on without you.
Life will never know how much it owes you,
The fighters of the field of war.

Worry in the field of war is immense,
But is put at the back of the mind.
It is true that life goes on,
But is it true that no worry is involved?
Worry is felt by the families of the fighters,
By the children, the wives and the parents.
Worry is felt by everyone deep down,
Whether they know it or not.

The people of this country owe so much to so few.
They feel so little towards the fighters.
The fighters of the field of war,
Once normal men now fighters to keep peace.
They fought with courage and pride.
They exist all around us if we only remember.

Alexandra Avern (12)
Edgbaston High School For Girls

Hopes And Fears Of The Homeless

The fears are yet to come
I shudder as I imagine
Mugged
Raped
Abused
Attacked
They're spinning round, round
Scared they're getting closer
No job
No money
No food
No clothing
The fear I dread gets closer
Closer still
Dying!

Hoping each day gets closer to;
A warm bed
Warm clothes
Warm bath
Oh how I wish
People who love me
Care about me
Dream on!
Food
Roast dinners
Presents on Christmas Day
A job
Family
All these wishes are in my head
My dreams.

Aimee McEvilly (13)
Edgbaston High School For Girls

MUSIC

Music is a beat, hip, hop and neat
The beats in the music want to make you dance
While you listen to music by Holly Valance
Westlife sing ballads so sweet
While Nelly sings to the roughest beat
Eminem's raps tell a story of his life
While P Diddy is singing for a wife
Pink rocks to 'Just like a pill'
While D12 sing on purple hills
Spice Girls ruled not for long
But Justin's intentions for Britney were wrong
Destiny's Child like being independent
While Blue's 'All Rise' are always dependent
Atomic Kitten like singing about boys
While Bob the Builder likes singing about toys
Music makes you move from side to side
The ones you like is for you to decide.

Anisha Parikh (13)
Edgbaston High School For Girls

IN THE SKY

I look through a telescope, what do I see?
A big blue background, with a cloud like a key.
The sky, the moon, the sun and stars,
All the planets, including Mars.
It's ever so blue in the sky,
You see the clouds passing by.
In the night the sun goes down
But in the morning it will rise.
The sky turns red as the day dies.

Francesca Schiller (11)
Edgbaston High School For Girls

AN ENGLISH LESSON

An English lesson does for me, always end up a catastrophe.
My teacher, who is called Mrs Brown, is always, always
wearing a frown.
When I put my hand up to ask how to spell 'celery',
She always tells me to look in a dictionary.
But what use is that? I'd eat my hat, if you ever, ever did find that.
So I checked all the 'Ss' time and time again
And eventually I asked her and she said, 'Jen,
I know you find it very hard, like trying and trying to stand on lard,
But if you look in the 'Cs' I'm sure you'll find it,' and she muttered,
'please!'
So I did as wily old Mrs Brown said and then I found my pot of gold
But how would I have found it if I wasn't told?!

Jennifer Mayhew (11)
Edgbaston High School For Girls

WINTER IN TOWN

Winter is a season that is cold like an iceberg crashing into a boat,
People ice skating on the pond like graceful swans swimming,
Chilling night sky like a blackboard shining,
The icy cold winds blow across the land like a blizzard,
Everyone is so quiet like an empty library,
Rabbits making finishing touches to their burrows
like busy bees around a hive,
Cold, shiny white snow covering bare trees,
Children outside having snowball fights on the streets,
Rain patters on my window like my heart beats,
White glistening everywhere,
Winter is here!

Rajni Farmah (11)
Edgbaston High School For Girls

LAST LESSON (IS ALWAYS BORING)

It t'was a horrible day
And in came our teacher Mrs Clay.
She shouted out in her big booming voice,
'Today girls I will give you a choice.
You're writing a poem!'

Paper was given
And things were written.
For over an hour,
Things were sour.
I was bored,
So I knotted the blind cord,
But then there was an idea,
That helped me see clear.

I wrote a page about a big cage,
But then the bell went
And we were sent.
Thank god it was the end of the day
And I have to say
Let's go and *play!*

Helen Graham (13)
Edgbaston High School For Girls

AUTUMN

A utumn is as red as fire.
U nderneath the carpet of leaves the grass remains untouched.
T rees are wearing beautiful bright coats.
U mbrellas blossom like blooming flowers.
M orning light, icy bright as a sapphire's glint.
N ext month comes winter as cold as the snow it brings.

Ella Peterman (11)
Edgbaston High School For Girls

WINTER

Early dark nights.
Fires aglow, roaring fiercely.
Icicles drooping down the windowpane.
Children waiting for Christmas Eve.

Outside, raining, pouring.
People hurrying home.
Children's cheeks bright red.

Christmas trees are up.
Schools have finished their first term.
It's getting colder.
At last Christmas is here.

Tonight is when Santa comes.
It's snowing heavily.
Morning comes at last,
Children open their presents,
Their faces surprised.

Sophie Ellis (11)
Edgbaston High School For Girls

WINTER

W inter wind blows, like a child blowing the candles out
on their birthday cake.
I ce on the roads, cars slipping and sliding, like penguins
with their flat flippers.
N ight sky is as black as a black cat's fur.
T rees are as bare as coat hangers, in an empty wardrobe.
E verybody is wearing warm clothes, like polar bears
with their thick layers of fur.
R ain is pouring as heavily as confetti at a wedding.

Anousha Hosseini (11)
Edgbaston High School For Girls

SCHOOL

In my same old uniform I walk to school
And I think wearing this I'll never be cool.

The same old colours blue, green and white,
It's too small for me so it looks really tight.

I haven't done my homework or the essay for today,
If the teacher finds out I'll never get away.

I walk through the doors that lead into school,
I know I'm looking like a right old fool.

I got two detentions and one D-merit,
I never for anything get any credit.

I'm so glad it's the end of the day,
I feel like screaming hip hip hooray!

Laura Foster (12)
Edgbaston High School For Girls

WINTER

Frost lies thick like white sheets over gardens.
Icicles stand as straight as soldiers.
It saddens me when I think of sunlight
Trying to scramble out of its darkened cage.
People wrapping up warm in woolly scarves.
But wait!
What's that in the distance?
Sunlight has returned.
Pushing away the winter,
Jumping merrily into the sky.

Laura Johnson (11)
Edgbaston High School For Girls

Daydreaming

The bell goes,
The teacher comes in,
I wonder where we will begin . . .

First we will go swimming with dolphins,
Under the crashing waves.
Oh no, one's stuck in-between some rocks,
I hope I can save him!

I hold my breath, open my eyes wide
And go down under.
I hold the shimmering flipper and tug,
I come back up and there's thunder.

What's that noise? I think it's the bell,
The teacher comes over and says,
'Where were you today, in bed?'

Rosie Maguire (12)
Edgbaston High School For Girls

My Cat

Trixey is my cat.
She's furry, black and fat.
She's never had a baby
So now she's gone all crazy.
She brings down socks in the morning
While everyone is snoring.
She wants the socks as kittens
But they're as still as dropped mittens,
Even though she moults her fur,
She knows we always love her!

Aimee Jarratt (12)
Edgbaston High School For Girls

WINTER

W ind howling at the windows like a wolf
I ncredible sky as black as coal
N ever-ending snow falls on the ground
T rees standing cold and lonely
E xtreme cold making you feel like a cold marble statue in a museum
R ain beating down as heavily as a waterfall.

Sinead McGeever (11)
Edgbaston High School For Girls

AUTUMN

A utumn is colourful like a rainbow
U mbrellas pop up just like an opening flower
T rees lose their leaves like rain falling
U npleasant cold creeps in like a snake
M ost people are playing with leaves
N early everyone is dressed up warm like a polar bear.

Hannah Bradley (11)
Edgbaston High School For Girls

AUTUMN

A utumn is bright like a rainbow in the sky
U p in the sky are clouds like grey cotton wool
T he leaves cover the ground like a colourful blanket
U mbrellas have opened like spring flowers
M any animals are hibernating like lazy people in bed
N ights grow longer like uncut hair.

Hannah Wishart (11)
Edgbaston High School For Girls

WINTER

W inter is like a giant snowball
I n winter the snow is like a white bed sheet
N eeding a scarf as warm as a tea cosy
T rees are covered in snow like icing on a bun
E very day is like a month
R oaring fires are like angry lions.

Ashley Smallwood-Rose (11)
Edgbaston High School For Girls

SUMMER

S andy beaches packed full.
U mbrellas out of use for a while.
M elting ice cream all over little children.
M um's putting sun cream on the whole family.
E ating strawberries and cream.
R ippling waves at the beach.

Harriet Layfield (11)
Edgbaston High School For Girls

WINTER

W inter is cold like an iceberg
I nside is warm just like a snug blanket
N ight's cloak is black like coal
T rees are bare like blank pieces of paper
E veryone is wrapped up like a polar bear
R ain and snow comes down like falling leaves.

Charlotte Yorke (11)
Edgbaston High School For Girls

Autumn

Early raindrops race down windows,
Pitter-pattering on rooftops.

Hard baked ground of summer
Covered with leaves, bronzed, golden.

Plentiful harvest brings fresh vegetables,
Lush red apples, crunchy carrots.

T-shirts turn to woollen jumpers,
Cold weak sun, breaks shivering clouds to cast long shadows.

Summer's hot, humid air,
Stirred by autumn's chilling breeze.

Spiders weave webs sparkling like diamonds,
Inside houses to escape the Jack Frost's spiky fingers.

Children playing merrily throughout summer
Sit by windows waiting for spring to come round again.

Summer fades away like
Colourful carnival dancers twirling away.

Trees, once abundant with bright green leaves,
Now bare as winter draws closer.

Summer's glowing hot sun
Now cold, pale as milk.

Georgia Clemson (11)
Edgbaston High School For Girls

HOLIDAYS

Suntan cream, sun glasses, spades, the lot!
Where to go, what to wear. I'm losing the plot.

The parks or the pool, I can't decide,
What about a walk or even the seaside?

On the beach there's a strong salty smell
Of the sand, the wind, seaweed and shells.

At the poolside, people diving and sliding
Under the water, spinning and gliding.

Back on the beach watching the sunset so shameless
The eternal sun so luminous and nameless.

Riding along on horseback in the countryside
The colours and mountains all flash by.

Back on the beach, back with smells,
Back with the weed and back with the shells.

Digging a hole, a castle, a moat,
Over the waves in a fast speedboat.

The wind in your hair, your hair in your eyes
The seagulls after fish as the day slowly dies.

Finally the end of this wonderful day
And sadly the end of my holiday!

Laura Kirby (12)
Edgbaston High School For Girls

SCHOOL

School starts early in the morning
Your alarm clock goes without any warning.

'Get up, get up, you sleepy head!'
Shouts Mum or Dad from the end of your bed.

'Come on, come on, we're going to be late!
Hurry up, it's already half-past eight!'

Up I get yawning away
Here goes another school day.

On goes the uniform without any care
I look in the mirror and brush my hair.

I hear the school bus drive away
God this is going to be a hell of a day.

A lecture by Dad about being on time
He makes it sound like I've committed a crime.

Sitting in maths paying no attention
I end the day with another detention.

Megan Stokes (12)
Edgbaston High School For Girls

ALL GROWN UP

We dream about
Being grown up,
Going to work
In our posh suits,
Driving a car
Down the M4
To find you have to
Teach a class of 24.

In a classroom
All day long,
Wishing you were
Somewhere else,
Doing another job.

Becky Simm (13)
Edgbaston High School For Girls

NO MORE FROM YOU

I've cried too many tears for you,
I'm happy now, life's fair and true.
No more thinking of you every day
I'm better without you anyway.

Laughed and smiled all the time,
That's how I mended this heart of mine.
I don't care about anything you do
Because I'm over you!

I gave you all my heart,
You just tore it apart.
No more tears and no more lies,
Now we've said our goodbyes.

Now she's hurt you, and,
You want me back to hold your hand.
You once caused me so much pain,
I won't be yours ever again.

No more confusing me,
No more using and abusing me.
You made me weak and now you see,
I've got all my girls supporting me.

Kate Haywood (13)
Edgbaston High School For Girls

The Seasons

Spring,
is a time of joy and happiness,
when new buds grow on the blossomed trees,
when new baby lambs are born
and new life is formed.

Summer,
it is hot,
when children go out to play on the luscious grass,
everyone and everything is beautiful and happy.

Autumn,
leaves turn brown and fall off the trees,
colourful leaves are caught up by autumn's sharp winds
and everyone is gathered indoors again.

Winter,
snow starts to form,
heating is suddenly needed,
because the cold is coming,
but there is one joy,
it's *Christmas!*

Sophia Angelides (13)
Edgbaston High School For Girls

Spring

S howers in April, puddles all around
P rimroses shooting up from underground,
R abbits hide from windy gales
I nteresting places on Easter egg trails
N ewborn lambs skipping high,
G rass freshly mowed under a pale blue sky.

Olivia Thomas (11)
Edgbaston High School For Girls

WHY?

The smell of fresh grass
going on for miles,
the soft petals of flowers
many colours,
the endless trail of birds
heading home.

Reality takes it away!

Endless trails of petrol fumes,
building sites that go on for miles,
roads that take over the country lanes,
no room for animals to survive.

That is reality!

I sometimes think to myself
it does not have to be like this.
But *why?*

Charlotte Smith (11)
Edgbaston High School For Girls

A POEM ABOUT KITTENS

K ittens love to play and jump
I n and out the cat flap with a bump,
T ossing, running in and out
T urn around and hear me shout
E ager to run away from
N aughty puppies out to play
S leeping, curled up in the hay.

Felicity Jones (13)
Edgbaston High School For Girls

HOMELESS

It's freezing outside, my fingers won't budge
Children are giggling as to school they trudge.
I look closer and squint my eye
They're giggling at me, oh I wish I could die.
Laughing and pointing and calling out names
Was I ever that cruel when I was their age?

My dad didn't want me, my mum didn't care
So I ran away with my teddy bear.
I have to beg and I have to steal
Always planning on how I'll get my next meal.
People snigger at me as they walk by,
To sleep at night, I have to cry.

No one to love me, to say I'll survive
No one to make me feel grateful that I'm alive.
I've spent most of my life on the street,
Learning from all the people I meet.

At night I close my eyes and dream,
Different flavours of ice cream
A mum that never wants to let me go!
But . . . my life will never be like this.

Sabah Babar (13)
Edgbaston High School For Girls

MY CAT . . .

My cat is like a tiger,
Ready for something to eat.
My cat is like a cheeky monkey,
Ready to scratch the seat.
My cat is like a lion,
Ready to pounce on whatever she finds.
My cat is like an evil cat,
When you pat her.

My cat is like a stupid thing,
Pouncing on the newspaper.
My cat is like a ball,
Falling on the floor.
My cat is like a human,
Eating whatever she can see.
My cat is like a fool,
Falling in the pool.

Elizabeth Gregory (11)
Edgbaston High School For Girls

CLOUDS

So calm, so peaceful, not a sound.
The clouds float high and gently round.
Without a care, a hope or hate
Never busy, never late.

White and fluffy, soft and round,
While children playing on the ground
Describe what each one means to them,
Whether it's cats or dogs, women or men.

They sit for hours thinking, dreaming,
About each cloud and its meaning.
About the people that they've seen
And the places that they've been
And things they only find in dreams.

As people carry on below,
Clouds above still come and go.
Some people, they will never know
What they're missing in the sky.

Rosamond Travers (13)
Edgbaston High School For Girls

If I Ruled The School

If I ruled the school every day would be the last of term
Every lesson would contain what you most wished to learn.
Every day would start at 10 and end at 3
Every day we will have time to watch TV.
Every match that was played would be a win for our team
Every picture that was painted would fulfil all dreams.
Every homework you got would be colouring fun
Everyday for break you'd have a chocolate bun.
Every exam you took would get you 100 per cent
Every essay you wrote would win the book event.
Everyone can play music with no ban
But me I prefer something from Catalan.
Every meal would be a superb cuisine
Every model you made would be a working machine.
Every computer would be easy to work
Everyone treated as equal not dirt.
Every term would be short, every holiday would be long
Every child would be taught cruelty is wrong.
If I ruled the school that's how it would be
But I can't make the rules for who'd listen to me?
I'm only the school cat but that's alright by me!

Amy Moore (13)
Edgbaston High School For Girls

The Ride

Life is like a ride.
When the ride stops you'll see the other side.
Sometimes it goes slow and sometimes fast,
But . . . it's never going to last.

The ride goes up and down,
It takes you all around,
The minute to think is here,
But it goes and then steps into fear.

When it all goes smooth it always plunges down,
I find myself in places out of bounds,
But I know I can't extend this ride,
For my fear I can't hide.

Shiza Khan (13)
Edgbaston High School For Girls

Daisy

Daisy, I want you to know,
I'll always be there for you,
I'll never ever leave,
Just keep me in your mind and you'll be in my heart,
Our friendship will achieve.

Daisy, we know each other so well,
That sometimes I believe,
That I am you and you are me
And we have as beautiful a friendship as can be!

Daisy, even when we're apart,
You're always on my mind,
Even if I go to Australia,
I would never leave you behind,
For you are like gold dust, the moon,
Better than any treasure find.

Daisy, your eyes glitter green, your freckles I know by heart,
Your speckly little legs make you run like a dart!
Daisy, lastly before I forget,
You're greater than great, as great as they get!
I know we've had our ups and downs,
But really on the whole,
We're the bestest of best friends,
Our friendship's as strong as a pole.

Maya Tankaria (11)
Edgbaston High School For Girls

WHO AM I?

When you look into my eyes,
What do you see?
Fear?
Hope?
When you reach into my heart,
What do you feel?
Happy?
Sad?
When you listen to my whispers,
What do you hear?
Spite?
Passion?
When you walk past me,
What do you smell?
Fragrance?
Radiance?
When you eat something I make
What do you taste?
Sweet?
Sour?
When you need a friend
Do you look for me?
Yes?
No?
Who am I?

Philippa Lilford (13)
Edgbaston High School For Girls

BEST FRIENDS

I never thought that you could be a friend,
So kind and thoughtful,
You make me laugh and sometimes cry,
It's then, that I feel awful,

But friendship lasts with those we love
And ours will last forever,
Whatever happens in our lives,
No one will part us ever!

Scarlett Pickering (12)
Edgbaston High School For Girls

The Beach At Sunset

Walking along the beach at sunset
The most magical time of the day
The wet golden sands glistening
In the remaining light of the sun.

The beach now empty, everyone gone
The traces of footprints fade away
The reminders of the hours before
Being slowly swept away
As the sea slowly creeps back up the beach,
Claiming the now deserted shore for itself again.

The once warm sands now cooling
In the gentle wind
Eventually being smothered
By the now mellow sea.
The remainders of sandcastles
Being slowly immersed in water
While leaving the slate clean for tomorrow.

The sunlight receding into
The now approaching dusk
The sky turning lavender
Against the golden velvet sands
And piece by piece the illuminated water
Fades away into the distance.

Bethan Moore (13)
Edgbaston High School For Girls

A JUMBLE OF ACTION AND SPEECH

Grumpy people moan,
Angry people shout,
Mental people scream abuse
And crash and tear about.

Quiet people mumble,
Happy people sing,
Vain people comb their hair
And adjust their ruby rings.

Hungry babies drool,
Protective mums fuss,
Late pupils run down roads
To try to catch the bus.

But I'm not like that,
Forgetful is my name
And this year I'm trying hard
To remember things again!

Hannah George (12)
Edgbaston High School For Girls

AUTUMN

Autumn winds fight me for my coat,
I grip tighter,
Freshly fallen leaves crackle beneath my feet,
Chilly air creeps slowly into my flesh,
Bare trees tower overhead,
Waiting, waiting,
Patiently waiting for warmer times,
My pace quickens as dark clouds circle above,
I reach shelter as raindrops bounce off pavements.

Charlotte Dean (11)
Edgbaston High School For Girls

Obsession With Colours

I love my mum
I really do
But the thing is
She's obsessed with blue.

All her rooms
Are like a deep blue sea
What's wrong with her?
What could it be?

Now the phase has passed
I'll remember to thank God it didn't last.

It's a different problem now
Oh enough said
Now she's got an obsession with *red!*

Nikita Joji (11)
Edgbaston High School For Girls

Winter Days

W inter is getting cold and dark
I n my warm, snug chair by the open fire.
N earer and nearer draws Christmas.
T hinking of all the presents on my list to Santa Claus.
E veryone rushing for last minute shopping.
R eady or not three days to go!

D ays are getting too slow to bear
A s Christmas comes closer,
Y es, only one night to go - how will I sleep?
S urprise! A sack full of presents just for me.

Kira Thompson (12)
Edgbaston High School For Girls

NAG, NAG, NAG

'Your room is like a pig sty.'
I really can't see why.
She nags me end on end
To vacuum every crack and bend.

Nagged again this morning,
That was my last warning.
'Mum, don't get so very mad,
It isn't really all that bad.'

'I really gotta go to school.'
'Do you take me for a fool?
We both know that it's Saturday.
You try my patience every way.'

I take a look around my lair.
Maybe it could use a little care.
Although I hate to write this down . . .
Forget it, I think I'm off to town.

Roshina Iqbal (11)
Edgbaston High School For Girls

THE WOOLLY WINTER

I woke up on Christmas Day,
Miles of white candyfloss all around,
Hedgehogs hibernating,
Birds flying,
All is silent.

As we passed the turkey around
Fire warming our toes up,
Church bells ringing,
Trees bare,
Get into the Christmas spirit.

Children having snowball fights,
Or building men out of snow,
Coldness tingles my toes,
People playing on sledges,
Shrieks and laughter are all you can hear.

Sophie Douglas (11)
Edgbaston High School For Girls

My Boring Life

My sister is a vampire,
She never goes to sleep.
My brother is a monkey,
He'll scream and shout and weep.
My mum's a shopaholic,
She just can't seem to stop,
My dad's an embarrassment,
He often blows his top!

My family altogether,
Is really down the drain.
It's even worse at school,
They all still use the cane.
We get a lot of homework,
It really is not fair.
The teachers are quite nasty,
They never seem to care.

My life is a misery,
I'll swap with anyone.
Although while I'm waiting,
My life will still go on!

Emily Clay (11)
Edgbaston High School For Girls

The Dreaded Exams

Exam, after exam, after exam.
There never seems to be a way out,
'We thought you said the test was next week!' we cry,
Begging our teachers for mercy.

'Revision is always the key,' our teachers tell us,
Knowing full well we will be disappointed with the results.
Do they take delight in watching us suffer?
Or deep down are they trying to help us?

When the exams come, everyone panics,
'Which side of the sheet were we meant to revise?'
'Do we have to know all these words?'
'I haven't revised, what am I going to do?'

It's time,
The exam papers are handed out.
We begin,
Knowing that this exam determines our future.

The teachers watch us and walk around the room,
Like the security guards, they were born to be.
Every move we make,
Is carefully noted.

Finishing the exam is the only way out,
It's the key to freedom,
All we have to do is complete it.

When we have finished, we give a sigh of relief.
It is over, we are free,
We have been released from the torturing exam paper
We are no longer prisoners of the exams.

Amanda Clarke (13)
Edgbaston High School For Girls

Angels

God's main assets
They are indeed
Helping those whatever their need.
Despite your disabilities
They'll always be there, guaranteed.

Life after death is
A serious matter
Although follows pain and suffering
Your angel will be there
To guide you through
Whatever the weather, rain or shine
You'll always find them there
Supporting you
Whatever your need.

Bringing hope to those now lost
Is a serious matter,
Only angels discuss
Helping people through grief and pain
The credit for that
Only angels can gain.

Guardian angels you will have
They may not have been shown to you yet
But soon they'll show themselves
One thing you must learn
However,
Is that not all angels
Are sent from
Heaven.

Vicky Hamilton-Jones (13)
Edgbaston High School For Girls

JOGGING IN THE AUTUMN

When the leaves turn red and orange
When the mornings are fresh and crisp
I wake up to the sound of birds,
Usually around six.

I peer out of my window
And feel the air on my face.
I leave my house and set a pace.

There is nobody else that I can see,
I start jogging and listen peacefully.
But then I feel the first few raindrops on my face.

The rain gets heavier and heavier
And I run faster and faster.

I reach home to where a bright fire glows
And I warm my fingers and toes.

Charlotte McCormack (13)
Edgbaston High School For Girls

WINTER

W inter is icy cold fingers touching your skin which make you shiver,
I s a whirling wind like screaming children eagerly waiting
for their presents,
N ativity plays are like a joyful herd of children trying their best,
T all Christmas trees sparkle like shining stars in the cold night sky,
E xcited children are like a roaring car engine,
R ain is like falling diamonds bouncing from the ground.

Julia Cheshire (12)
Edgbaston High School For Girls

IN THE JUNGLE

In the jungle lions growl,
In the jungle panthers prowl,
In the jungle monkeys dance,
In the jungle crocodiles glance.

In the forest a gentle breeze,
In the forest pine trees,
In the forest a nightingale sings,
In the forest birds spread their wings.

By the sea jagged rocks,
By the sea boats at the docks,
By the sea waves lap the shore,
By the sea seagulls screech for more.

On the hills the wind blows my hair,
On the hills a galloping mare,
On the hills green grass,
On the hills a stream like glass.

On a moor pretty flowers,
On a moor April showers,
On a moor a squelchy bog,
On a moor a deer in fog.

In the city rushing around,
In the city not a jungle sound,
In the city all is grey,
In the city no trees to sway,
In the city building blocks,
In the city empty docks,
In the city shop tills,
In the city you can't see the hills,
In the city traffic roars,
In the city far away from green moors.

Kirsty Purnell (11)
Edgbaston High School For Girls

HALLOWE'EN

Hallowe'en is a spooky day,
It's celebrated in an old-fashioned way,
Witches upon broomsticks, pumpkins galore,
Spiders crawling on the floor.

Ghosts come out the graveyard at night
And try to give you a terrible fright,
Vampires who like mortal blood,
Sneak around with their black hood.

Children dressed for Hallowe'en,
Which they enjoy and make a scene.
They knock on the door, 'Trick or treat?'
And people give them sweets to eat.

But if they turn you away at the door,
Beg on the floor until they give you some more,
If you don't get any treats,
Move onto one next street.

At the end of the night,
After everyone has had a fright,
The ghosts return to the graveyard after causing fear
And won't be back until next year.

Gursharan Rai (13)
Edgbaston High School For Girls

I WILL WAIT FOR YOU

When I'm in Heaven and you're down below,
I will never let you go.
I will tell the other angels your name,
I would wait for you until you came.
Our friendship will shine for evermore,

I'll be waiting by that golden door.
You'll be carrying that golden key,
It will lead you back to me.
Then we will be united again,
Our friendship will still be the same.

Niquita Pilgrim (12)
Edgbaston High School For Girls

One Day

It was a day when things went wrong
and disaster struck.

My mum was stuck in a jam
because a man had crashed his van.

My little sister was getting impatient
because she wanted chocolate.

She's only four but I was tired
from a long day at school
and I couldn't be bothered
to walk over the road.

She left my side and
let go of my hand and
then I heard a *crash!*
A woman climbed out of her car
and screamed when she saw what she'd done.

There was my little sister lying
down as though she was asleep.
Then, I feared for her life,
but now she's fine as can be,
but I think how careful we must be.

Camilla Walt (13)
Edgbaston High School For Girls

Winter

First day of winter
Freezing cold
A white sheet covers the leaves,
That are now
Brown,
Not gold.

Moving along,
Hallowe'en
Children can be heard
But monsters
Seen.

Whizzing through the season,
Bonfire Night!
Rainbows of colours,
Flames so bright,
Amazing,
Look at Guy Fawkes!

At last
Christmas Day,
Santa's come,
In an exciting way,
Opening presents,
What's this?
Brilliant,
This is bliss.

Gemma Doswell (11)
Edgbaston High School For Girls

THE LONELY GHOST

The stars are large and bright
And were gleaming
With a silvery light
And a beautiful night,
When a shadowy figure
Opened the door,
Of an old closed up house
And as her feet touched the floor
They left no footprints
On the dusty boards,
For this girl one day
Went down to the park,
So that she could play
But back . . . she never came.

And now every night
At 12 o'clock
She opens the door
And steps inside,
But further in
She cannot go
For her spirit is trapped
So she takes one last
Mournful look
At the familiar surroundings
Before she returns
Shedding silent tears
Back to her grave.

Joanna Champion (11)
Edgbaston High School For Girls

IF ONLY I'D LOOKED AFTER MY TEETH

Oi, what's that squirty thing?
Take that sharp thing away,
Remove those big pliers,
You'll play for this, you'll pay!

I'm lying on the dentist's chair,
Mouth open wide,
Dentist fiddling, nurse smiling
And Mum's by my side.

If only, if only I say to myself,
If only I'd looked after my teeth.
And looked in the mirror and brushed them each day,
I'd have spotted the perils beneath.

If only I'd eaten in the kitchen
And not hidden chocolate under my bed.
If only I hadn't spent my money in the sweetie shop,
I could have saved it all up instead.

If only I'd used my new toothbrush
And been just that bit much more willing,
Cut down on the junk, and watched what I drunk,
I would have much more teeth than filling.

If only I'd listened to Mum,
Rather than stand there and yawn.
If only I'd listened to a word that she'd said
And put down that extra one scone.

If only I'd looked after my teeth
And given it that little bit of thought,
I wouldn't be lying here, mouth open wide, with Mum by my side,
All the lectures I've had, to think the times I've been taught.

If only I'd looked after my teeth!

Laura Bleetman (13)
Edgbaston High School For Girls

Snow

Snow is like white powder,
Children like to play in it and make snowmen,
A carrot for the nose,
Two buttons for the eyes,
A few buttons for the mouth,
Two twigs for the arms,
A hat and scarf to keep it warm.
The snow is like a white blanket,
You can make snow angels,
But when you get up
They always go wrong.
Come on kids, it's time for tea,
Now go to bed,
You wake up in the morning,
Look out of the window,
But sadly the snow is gone.

Bobbie Blair (11)
Edgbaston High School For Girls

An Hour

You can spend it at a bus stop,
Spend it down in town,
Spend it in a station or even in a crowd,
You can spend it at a party,
Spend it in the bath,
Spend it in the shower,
Or even with your staff!
You could spend it on your settee,
Or watching the television,
You could use one while you're sleeping,
Or 3 or 4 or 5,
Or use it at the cinema,
While eating a popcorn pot.
You couldn't use an hour,
For a holiday, Christmas or a birthday,
Use it quick, no time to lose,
However you use it, you can choose.

Jo Parker (13)
Edgbaston High School For Girls

Hurricane!

H urtling around smashing trees,
U prooting flowers from their beds,
R ipping through tall buildings,
R ound and round it spins,
I llusions are created as death is near,
C an nobody stop this beast?
A nimals flee, the ground is shaking!
N ever stopping wind, grinding up the earth.
E verything is still.

Katy Blunt (11)
Edgbaston High School For Girls

HOMELESSNESS

The rain pours down in icy sheets,
Drenching me to the skin,
My cardboard box providing no protection,
From the bitter wind which cuts through me
And chills me to the bone,
I'm starving but I can't get food,
Maybe I could try those bins over there?
I scavenge through them like a wild hungry-eyed fox,
Nothing,
I make in the direction of a subway,
My lucky day!
The old newspaper serves as a good blanket,
I huddle up against the wall, tired and famished,
My last thoughts before sleep clouds my mind are,
Who cares about me anymore? No one.
Homelessness is not a crime, people think only animals live this way.

Claudia Burnand (11)
Edgbaston High School For Girls

A BROKEN HEART

Tears are shedding from your eyes,
You cannot hide your desperate cries,
Alone in the house once more,
You keep on staring at the door.
Oh he'll be back I know he will but why
Not now for I am waiting for my man.
Farewell he said as he left the room,
As it is not you who wins my heart,
With that he closed the door
And broke my heart even more.

Lucy Cole (12)
Edgbaston High School For Girls

WHAT CAN YOU DO WITH A BOOK?

You can read it
Or hit someone on the head,
Read it in the bath or in bed.

Use it to steady a chair
Take it with you to the fair,
Trap it in the door
Or slam it on the floor.

Make a shape in some sand,
Balance it on your hand,
Lean it against the wall,
Take it and sell it in the mall.

Use it to rest your head,
Rip the pages out instead,
Cover it up with some paper,
Read about how lambs caper.

There is so much more you can do with a book,
If you take a closer look.

Gurkirat Hayer (13)
Edgbaston High School For Girls

SWEETS, SWEETS

I wish the world was made of sweets!
Houses of Mars would be really neat!
Chairs of marshmallows and Snickers galore,
Beds of Maltesers and Rolos I adore!
Wine gums for breakfast and jellybeans for tea,
Lunch is some gummies for my friend and me,
When it's Christmas gummy worms are nice,
Miniature Heroes would fill up my plate twice.

A top made from Buttons and a candyfloss shirt,
A bit more here and there, should not hurt,
I write with a pen of liquorice stick!
As I do my homework the pen I start to lick!
I wish the world was made of sweets,
Sweets around us would make nice treats!

Lindsey Hunt (12)
Edgbaston High School For Girls

Why Did I Do It?

Pick up a pen,
Running like the wind,
Head aching like mad,
Wishing I had never done it.

She comes towards me,
She's overtaking me now,
Tells me the time,
As she rushes by.

I start to get scared,
As I look around,
She's way in front of me now,
She is the worst of them all.

I have not told my mum,
My friends will stand up for me,
I should not be doing this,
Why did I do it?

Times up,
I get out second,
My mum's standing at the gate,
I promise I will never run again.

Emma Walford (13)
Edgbaston High School For Girls

MOVING HOUSE

Moving house was such a big chore!
I found lots of things I never knew I had before!
I went through the loft, wardrobe and drawers,
Finding toys that I had when I was four!
When everything was packed, I was ready to go,
I was really upset, but would not let it show!

The removal van pulled up outside,
I stopped myself, before I cried.
I held back my tears and my throat was dry,
As I stepped in the car and whispered, 'Goodbye.'
All my life I had lived there, for over twelve years,
Shared my desires and secrets, hopes and fears.

The journey progressed, not far to go,
Just half a mile away to our new home!
I opened the door of our new house
And crept upstairs, like a visiting mouse,
What happens next, I really can't say?
I've only just got here . . .
Today's the day!

Laura Payne (12)
Edgbaston High School For Girls

SHOES

I love shopping, especially for shoes,
When I come back empty-handed I get the blues,
Sandals, platforms and trainers too,
I love every kind of shoe.

I quite like Pod, Sketchers are cool,
I have to have the latest shoes, or I'll look a fool!
Red or Dead is a wicked make
And I love my pair of Prada even though they're fake.

Clogs and boots and gorgeous pink flip-flops,
How do I choose out of so many shops?
There's Shelly's, Dolcis and Ravel too,
Oh how I love every kind of shoe!

Viki Harrison (12)
Edgbaston High School For Girls

What Is It?

Oh thanks Nan, wonderful present,
It's got a lovely horn,
Nice trunk too
And hundreds of things it can do,
Lots of buttons,
A big brass knob,
A good job,
It's wearing a football kit,
It's nice Nan but what is it?

Oh thanks Nan, nice pressie,
It looks like a train,
Could be a plane,
Maybe a jumbo jet,
Look somewhere to sit,
It is nice nan but what is it?

Oh thanks Dad, I think,
(This is getting silly)
It has got what looks like a broken TV
Hundreds of sweets
And other yummy stuff to eat,
A book to read,
A funny looking millipede,
A boxing thing to hit,
It's nice Dad but what is it?

Elizabeth Ingamells (13)
Edgbaston High School For Girls

A NEW SCHOOL

Going to a brand new school
Can make you feel blue.
It all seems very scary
And you don't know what to do.

Walking down the corridor,
With no place to go.
You stand trembling, thinking,
'When is it time to go?'

People rush past you,
Sweeping you away,
Laughing, joking, chatting,
But you don't know what to say.

When you're in the classroom
And the teacher comes your way,
You sit quietly working
And hope she goes away.

Breaktime is approaching,
You begin to worry,
Most people run off,
In a frantic hurry.

When you think you're all alone
And you'll have to sit on your own,
A group of girls come up to you
And kindly offer to sit with you.

Soon enough you're the best of friends,
You don't want school to end!
It's not so bad after all,
Running through those crowded halls.

So when you start at a new school,
Just remember to keep your cool!

Naomi Patel (13)
Edgbaston High School For Girls

NOTHING BUT A DREAM . . .

Here I was far from home
In a place I never knew
In front of me the night still young
I saw a candle next to me
Its light flickering in this restless night,
In the candle I saw a light of hope,
But why do I see such visions?
Then a warm fuzzy feeling swept into me
For an unexplainable reason.
All of this I can't perceive,
I felt myself soaring through the air,
Looking down below at this
Illuminated wondrous place below.
Then abruptly it all started to blur away
I found myself falling far below
And lo, here I am at home, but I
Don't understand,
Was it nothing but a dream?

Manasi Jyothish (11)
Edgbaston High School For Girls

Life's Train

I stand there on the platform,
Looking at the train go by,
I then say to myself,
Maybe I should give life another try.

So, I jump on the train,
Going oh, so very slow,
Then the train gets quicker,
Now my life is at a normal flow.

I hardly even notice,
Time soon flies by,
Now I'm happy and glad,
That I gave my life another try.

Anny Yousef (12)
Edgbaston High School For Girls

My Hamster Is . . .

My hamster is like a racing car
rushing around her cage.
My hamster is like a sprinter
when she runs inside her wheel.
My hamster is like a furry ball
when she is fast asleep.

My hamster is like a vacuum cleaner
eating everything she can.
My hamster looks like a giant pufferfish
when she fills her pouches with food.
My hamster sounds like a pneumatic drill
when she bites the cage to file her teeth.

Laura Grindulis (11)
Edgbaston High School For Girls

Field Trip

Going on a field trip,
You have to stop and stare,
You cannot tell which is which,
The teacher or the bear.

She growls so loud,
She stands up tall
And for the first time in all your life,
You wish you were at school.

You're dripping wet, you can't go on,
The lion tells you to, 'Shut up!'
'But it's January Miss!
Can't we go in June?'

You have to look at all the rocks
And if you dare to ask,
'What's so interesting about pebbles, Miss?'
She'll look at you, aghast.

'These are not just pebbles girls!
They are called scree!'
And before long, you find your head,
Is resting on your knee.

And even worse, she tells you to be smart,
'You're representing the school,'
And then, the silly woman leads you,
Through a muddy pool!

Sophie Price (13)
Edgbaston High School For Girls

BIRTHDAYS

Rush down the stairs,
Like running from bears,
You're flushed with excitement.

Your head filled with joy,
When you unwrap your first toy,
But you suddenly turn low,
When you find out, it's from Auntie Flo.

The next toy's from Mum,
When you get some chewing gum,
The day is the best,
But when you get home,
You just want to rest.

Birthdays are fantastic,
The best day of them all,
But at the end of the day,
You're always glad, it's out of the way.

Emily Hiley (13)
Edgbaston High School For Girls

RAIN

Many people don't like the rain,
Instead of walking, they take the train,
They moan out loud,
When they see a cloud,
Many people don't like the rain.

Many people don't like the rain,
Especially when they're walking down the lane,
They get in a muddle,
When they step in a puddle,
Many people don't like the rain.

Many people don't like the rain,
They think it's a real pain,
They get in a tizzy
And their hair goes all frizzy,
Many people don't like the rain.

Charlotte Clemson (13)
Edgbaston High School For Girls

AUTUMN

A corns, conkers, crispy leaves and yellow leaves,
U ntil cold, icy winter comes our way.
T reasures of yellow and treasures of red,
U nique colours of leaves float to the ground,
M y feet lay inches away from them,
N eatly placed there like pictures with no meaning.

Nicola Reid (11)
Edgbaston High School For Girls

SUMMER

S uncream smells in the air,
U nder the blue sky I lie,
M arigolds like butter, spring from the ground,
M ilkshakes being supped in every cafe,
E veryone's out in the garden trying to get a tan,
R ed rosy cheeks as they bake in the sun.

Romilly Smith (11)
Edgbaston High School For Girls

AUTUMN

Leaves sway on trees like rusty gates,
Autumn's blanket of beauty has fallen on our world;
Red, orange, yellow.
Crisp leaves crackle underfoot,
Autumn's leaves fall from everywhere; sun and sky.
Crimson carpets across speckled ground.
This time of year again;
Warmth fading,
Fleeing from inevitable winter.
Colours dominate all,
Dullness banished,
As if forever by autumn,
Bronzed conkers,
Peacock sky; time of colour,
Autumn
Season of independence.

Katie McClughen-Tate (11)
Edgbaston High School For Girls

THINGS TO DO WITH A BOOK

You could pack it snug
Inside a bag,
Cover it with a dirty rag,
Read a chapter, put it down,
The man that wrote
It was a clown.
Cover it with shiny paper,
Goodness me, what a caper.

Maybe try to take it back
And attempt to get your money back,
Shove it hard behind a bookcase
Or
Lie it flat on its face,
If you have an unsteady table,
Prop it up, if you are able.

Sophie Blight (14)
Edgbaston High School For Girls

What Can You Do With A Cup?

You can break a candle,
Paint her blue as the sea,
Then crack the handle,
Use her for steaming tea,
Or coffee for when it snows,
Use as an instrument,
To balance on your nose,
Or water to lament.
Pair up with a saucer,
Tap on a table
And take a sip out of her,
Then crack using a ladle,
To slide across the floors,
Put her on a stand,
Trap between the doors
And hold it in your hand!

Jamilla Jack (14)
Edgbaston High School For Girls

AUTUMN'S AN IRISH SETTER

Autumn stirs stretching her legs,
As she wags her tail, leaves begin to fall,
Summer has gone.
Her rusty leaves frolic in brisk winds,
Laughing as they dance around.
Running fast over hills,
She deposits layers of red fur on
Woodland after woodland,
Bounding around,
Not a care for poor Summer,
Exiled for another year.
Her coat of many golden leaves,
Glistens as fading light catches it,
Eyes gleaming mischievously.

Rebecca Tatlow (11)
Edgbaston High School For Girls

THE SEASONS OF THE RAIN

Rain, rain, autumn rain,
Autumn rain, leading cold,
I despise the rain as cold as ice,
Which comes again.

Rain, rain, winter rain,
Winter air, unexciting and dark,
I hate the rain, pouring in the drain,
Which comes again.

Rain, rain, spring rain,
Spring rain urging bloom,
I like the rain, filled with life,
Which comes again.

Rain, rain, summer rain,
Summer rain, growing grass,
I enjoy the rain that keeps me happy,
Which comes again.

Esther Dasol Lee (13)
Edgbaston High School For Girls

PROMISE

As I wave Danielle goodbye
I promised I would return,
But would I, I didn't know,
I don't think anyone did,
All I'd been told was I was going to serve my country.
I didn't want to leave my wife
And our six-month-old baby.
Could they cope alone?
Would they forget me?
If I became one of the millions
Of unidentified bodies in a foreign land.
Would I be captured by the Nazis
And killed at gunpoint?
Could I keep my promise?
I didn't know.

Michél Ward (13)
Edgbaston High School For Girls

WINTER DAYS

Now skies are dull,
Just like watercolour paintings,
Storm clouds are coming back from holidays abroad,
They are already playing nasty tricks.

Sharp, biting winds,
With pins, daggers,
Bee stings and wasps,
Torturing my body right through.

Snowflakes as hard as rock,
Fly at the speed of light towards my face,
Making my stubby fingers turn scarlet,
My runny cherry tomato nose becomes even more ruby.

My hair flicks, wildly back upon my face,
Umbrellas spring upside down to irritate their owners,
Scarves flying out of reach of their freezing necks,
Gloves heavy with wet snow.

Wickedness, harsh punishment,
It's hard to take steps in this chaos
Of blustery winds, heavy snow
Nobody deserves this!
I'll be glad to reach my comfortable, warm home.

My key, stiff with cold, slowly turns to unlock my door,
As I walk in, warm air stings my face,
Delightful smells of winter casserole welcomes me home,
I've only been down to the corner shop!

Ellie Coe (11)
Edgbaston High School For Girls

FOR THE LAST TIME IN MY LIFE

As I watch the sunset
Dying away like my soul,
I think of the times I spent with my friends
And how, when separated, we never seemed whole.

I remember all the joyous days,
In which we laughed together,
Screaming on the theme park rides,
Or running through fresh heather.

Now those times have come and gone,
To be replaced by hardship,
We have been put in difficult situations,
But they have not torn our friendship.

The years have passed and we have grown,
But still deep in my heart,
The thought remains that you loved me,
From the bottom of your heart.

I wonder if I'll see you again,
So I just want to say,
Thank you for what you've done for me
And I love you to this day.

The ruby-red fills the sky,
Mixing with the blue,
It makes me think about my life
And how much I'll miss you.

Sayyida Mehrali (12)
Edgbaston High School For Girls

A Christmas Dream

Lying there,
Glowing, white icicles falling all around me,
All shapes, all sizes,
I sat up,
I looked back,
No green grass in sight,
Just white,
White, glittering blanket,
I smelt something,
What was it?
Another scent surrounded me,
Christmas pudding I thought,
Slowly, I lay back down and heard
The ground crunch beneath me,
As I looked up, I realised the stars
Had come out,
Something about them made me shiver,
My eyes rolled further back in their sockets,
Colourful branches swayed as the wind blew,
Some light, some warmth, came from them,
My hands felt like ice cubes stuffed in wool,
I felt my eyelids droop as I started to think,
I thought of presents and the food awaiting,
Christmas was only tomorrow,
I never knew,
Did I fall asleep?
I opened my eyes,
Bright rays shone around me,
Then it struck me,
Today was Christmas Day.

Khyati Modgil (11)
Edgbaston High School For Girls

SUBMARINE

I was having fun in my submarine when
Charlie came to play,
He looked at the sub and said,
'Wow, can I go in your nightclub?'
My little sister came to me and asked,
'Is that pony there for me?'
As the day went on my sub became,
A car,
A house,
A train,
A plane,
The day went on more people came,
The submarine continued to change,
An elephant,
A motorbike,
It didn't stop there, it then became,
A time machine,
A spaceship,
An eagle in the sky,
The fun went on for two more days,
The changing sub lived on and on.
A warship,
A theatre,
A castle,
A cloud.
Nothing could ruin the fun but . . .
'Mum, where's my submarine?' I asked one day.
'What?'
'The one in the corner of the room,'
'Oh that old cardboard box . . . I needed it!'

Sarah Norris (13)
Edgbaston High School For Girls

Retinablastoma

R eal or artificial
E yes, I have a lot
T ears of sorrow
I wonder where it's gone
N ever to be able to see through my right eye
A gony to cope through school
B usy little bee I am
L earning everything I can
A ngry through the past eleven years
S pecial and unique
T winkle, it does not give
O nly one eye to see through
M other is very upset
A nd all of this was because of
Retinablastoma.

Tiffany Pang (13)
Edgbaston High School For Girls

My Friend

Her hair is a flickering fire,
Her eyes are blue sapphires,
Her lips are always grinning,
She's hardly ever sinning,
She's quite good at swimming,
But she isn't always winning,
She's quite long and lean
And she likes toffee ice cream,
She likes playing the fool
And tries to keep school rules,

She's quite creative (that's for sure)
Her heart really is quite pure,
If she ever left me,
I'd be lost in a big, wide sea.

Hannah Lewis (11)
Edgbaston High School For Girls

BEST FRIENDS FOREVER

B eing together is so cool,
E verything is according to rules,
S eeing each other every day
T ells us that we will play.

F inding that you're here now,
R eminds me that you're not a cow,
I n every way you're the best,
E verytime I see a bird's nest.
N obody tells me that you're bad,
D evil only,
S ays you're sad.

F riends we'll always be,
O nly you and of course, me,
R etelling stories from the past,
E very time just like the last,
V ampires make me scared,
E veryone says they're
R are!

Aleya Abdul Ali (12)
Golden Hillock School

Cats Are Cute

C ats are cool in the face,
A ren't they cute with a smile?
T alented enough to speak,
S creech loudly but simply know how to creep.

A nd even they play together,
R eact to help their mother,
E at enough to hug their father.

C ute enough to mess around,
U nderground they play games because they love the ground,
T hey become very sleepy and want to cry,
E very day have a bath but never stay dry.

Rehana Rasool (13)
Golden Hillock School

Little Man

There was a little man
His chest, hairy and brown,
His eyes are little,
His ears are big,
With the longest nose in the town,
There was a little man,
Who had a frying pan,
He battered up the boys,
Who stole his cuddly toys
And they never dared to come back again,
The boys went to the man again
And stole his frying pan and cuddly toy
And they ran away and left the man crying behind.

Rudauha Ferdes (11)
Golden Hillock School

All About Flowers

A ll the
F lowers
S hould
H ave
E ven an
E nding
N o way

N ever
I t's
Z ebra
A t
K ate's garden
A nd
T ea together!

Afsheen Nizakat (11)
Golden Hillock School

Friendships

Friendships will die
With arguments and lies
I know how it feels 'cause it happened to me,
Like ashes to dust
Turned our trust
Into something unpleasant and mean.
Avoiding each other
One day after another
As guilt became easy to see
I know it's my fault, as my teacher made me realise
So the very next day, I went to apologise
I'm glad now our friendship is the way it's supposed to be.

Shapla Begum (13)
Golden Hillock School

Golden Hillock School

We are the kids from Golden Hillock School,
Don't you know that we're so cool?
We're from Sparkhill, we're no fools,
That is why we love our school.

England, Bangladesh and Pakistan,
That is where we come from man!
Just like food in the frying pan,
We mix it up like no one can.

North, east, south or west,
That's why they say we're the best,
We always pass our English tests,
We are better than all the rest.

Monir Uddin (12)
Golden Hillock School

What Is Love?

Love could be anything,
If you mean what you're saying,
He may love you, she may love you,
What is love?

With friends you have a special bond,
It may be love you never know,
Have you ever felt like that?
What is love?

Roses, rings and dinners,
Maybe this is love, yes maybe it's love,
Your heart is only filled with one name,
What is love? Oh, what is love?

Fatheha Naznin (12)
Golden Hillock School

THE SCHOOL TOILETS

The school toilets are very scary,
Many children go there, sizes vary.

The only people who hang out there are the big boys,
Not small, little kids who still play with toys!

The toilets are always smelling of smoke,
I wouldn't go there even if I was provoked.

There's one kid who rules it all,
He's the oldest there and very tall.

Kids are bullied there nearly every day,
I hope I'm not next, that's all I pray!

I never go near there, whatever I do,
In case I get my head flushed down the loo!

Zahed Hussain (13)
Golden Hillock School

LIFE

Life is like a river,
It flows calm and slow,
There are different paths in life,
Which we decide to take.
We only live once in life,
In life we have good and bad times
Which we can't avoid,
Life doesn't come and go,
It stays with us forever,
Treat life good
And life will treat you good in return!

Shaflo Akhtar (14)
Golden Hillock School

PLAYGROUNDS

Playgrounds are such gobby places,
Know what I mean?
Everyone seems to have something to talk about,
Giggle, whisper, scream, gossip and shout about,
I mean, it's like being in a parrot cage!

And playgrounds are such pushy places,
Know what I mean?
Everyone seems to have to run about,
Jump, kick, do cartwheels, handstands and fly around,
I mean it's like being in a whirlwind.

The clatter of the shoes of teachers,
The laughter of the kids and creatures,
The idiotic behaviour of the 5th years,
Know what I mean?
It's like you're the only one that's down to earth!

Girls gossiping about the rumour they heard,
Boys muttering about, 'That maths teacher's a nerd!'
Teachers running into the staffroom for their revolting coffee,
While I stand and chew at my last toffee.

I mean when you ask the senseless Big-Bob the bully
What does motivation mean?
Immediately 'motorcycle' would pop into his pathetic head,
Which would pile up my lack of frustration,
I mean it's like 'get a life.'

Playgrounds are such pally places,
Know what I mean?
Everyone seems to have best friends,
Secrets, link arms, be in gangs, have a laugh!
Everyone, except me,

Know what I mean?

Sultana Sheikh (14)
Golden Hillock School

What Is An Inspiration To You?

Love is an inspiration to me,
Because it can mean a lot of things.
If there isn't any love in the world,
Then what can there be?

Love is everything you mean to me, or
Love is nothing you mean to me.
Love is friendship between you and me,
Capture it in my hand and never let it flee.

Hearts can be broken so how can you survive?
Drowning your sorrows with no one alive,
Happiness or sadness, to be or not to be,
What will it be?

Love is an inspiration to me,
Because it means a lot of things,
If there isn't any love in the world,
Then what can there be?

Rubina Mukul (12)
Golden Hillock School

Seasons

W aking up to see snow,
I cy paths, snowy tops,
N ot to worry, stay inside warm,
T rying to go and play with snow,
E ager to make snowmen,
R olling over, immense snowball covering you.

A nd out comes the sun,
N ow you know,
D own the silence.

S pring is finished,
U p goes the sun,
M erry, merry in people's houses,
M other's telling children to wear suntan oil,
E verything is so exciting,
R ound, round go the seasons.

Mohammed Silman (12)
Golden Hillock School

Star

If I were a star,
I would twinkle all day,
Guiding you to the right way,
I would be there every day and night,
Giving you light,
Being your best mate,
Having so much faith in you,
Oh a star, a star,
A far, far,
Star.

Khurrum Bader (12)
Golden Hillock School

FRIENDSHIP

A friend is *f*unny and *f*antastic,
A friend is *r*espectful and *r*esponsible,
A friend is *i*nteresting and *i*ntelligent,
A friend is *e*xciting and *e*ntertaining,
A friend is *n*eat and *n*earby,
A friend is *d*elightful and *d*ependable,
A friend is *s*afe and *s*ound.

Nasir Arshad (11)
Golden Hillock School

SCHOOL

S chool is boring
C oncentrating on work makes me end up snoring
H ave to wake up in the morning, makes me feel tired
O ne of the teachers even got fired
O ne by one the lessons pass by
L earning new things and listening to girls cry

Mehran Kaiser (12)
Golden Hillock School

AUTUMN

Having lots of fun in the autumn,
Autumn makes leaves turn crisp and gold,
Birds stop singing in the cold.
In the night, water falls.
Birds come out and fly to the ground,
At last, autumn has come.

Habiba Begum (11)
Golden Hillock School

SEASONS

Leaves falling, children playing,
Autumn is on its way!

Wind howling, snow falling,
Snowball fights everywhere!

Flowers rising, sun ascending,
Spring cleaning everywhere!

Flowers grown, sun is out,
Summer clothes appearing everywhere!

Sonia Akhtar (12)
Golden Hillock School

FRIENDSHIP

Good friends are for sharing.
They care deeply for you.
When you are feeling down and out,
They give you laughing to do!

They buy you pressies to open
On your birthday,
Which make you cry with happiness
And make you glad all day.

So always remember friends,
Whenever you're feeling sore,
Because they'll be there to help you out,
That's what friends are for!

Samantha Fitzgerald (12)
Hillcrest School

The Midnight Poem

Dark and scary, creepy shadows,
Could be a monster, it could be anything.
Screaming, shaking, what's going on?
I'm scared the monster's going to get me!
He's getting closer, what is it?
I'm going to die,
Help me someone.
Mom, Dad, where are you?
Help!
Silence . . .
Oh good, it was all a dream.

Sarah Minks (12)
Hillcrest School

Leaving Home

I'm free, free
out here on my own,
having to look out for myself.
I'm at college now,
I'm so excited at meeting new friends,
But at the same time, I'm scared,
Scared that I might need my mom
And she won't be there.
What if I can't go home
And I get homesick?
What if?

Lyndsey Smith (13)
Hillcrest School

One Year

It's been one year now,
One year since they came.
Slowly I fall and I'm left in this pain.

It's been one year now,
One year since they took you away.
These thoughts are making me insane.

It's been one year now,
One year since you left me and this place.
I'm so scared I might forget your face.

It's been one year now,
One year without you by my side.
It's been this long since the day you left and made me cry.

It's been one year now,
One year since you went away and died.
One year and I never got the chance to say goodbye.

Atrin Nejad (16)
Hillcrest School

Fire

I am the fire,
I am strong and bright,
In the night you can see my light.
My red-hot flame burns slowly,
But enough to make the sky warm.

People think I am fierce,
But no one knows what I am really like.
I warm people's homes,
I keep people out of the cold,
My flame will never grow old.

I can fight through rain and wind,
I am powerful, like a king.
Remember my flame is always there,
I might look frightful, but I do really care.
I am the fire!

Helen Savage (13)
Hillcrest School

AUTUMNAL NIGHTMARE

Blood-red eyes,
Harrowing cries,
Rustling leaves,
Misty seas.

Wolves run and howl
At the moon,
Dogs bark and growl,
They'll chase me soon.

Blood-red eyes,
Harrowing cries,
Rustling leaves,
Misty seas.

Something pounces,
It's on me, growling,
Wolves are prowling,
I'm crying . . .

Perhaps I'm dying?
But now I'm sighing,
It was just a scare,
A nightmare,
But . . . those eyes seem familiar!

Anna-Marie Averill (13)
Hillcrest School

WHEN I'M OUT PLAYING

When I'm out playing,
There're lots of fun things to do,
You can play with the skipping rope,
Or you can play with the ball,
But even better, you can play knock-door-run.
Lots of children like to play that game
Because they think it's good when they get a chance.
I don't like the game knock-door-run,
I just like to sit and talk,
But much better, lie down and sleep,
That would keep me occupied, rather than being bored.
Sometimes we go and climb a tree
Where the tree house is, to have some fun.
Sometimes we go on a hunting run
To see if we can find some bugs,
And even funnier, on our bikes
Up and down the BMX track.
Even up at the park with my little sister.
She would love to go up to the park every day
And play on the swings and slide,
But I couldn't take her every day
Because it's much to far to walk.
I like playing out with my friends and brothers and sisters,
It's so much more fun than sitting in my room on my own.

Gemma Thomas (12)
Hillcrest School

SUNLIGHT

As soon as the sunlight hits my window, I know it's morning.
As soon as the sunlight hits my window, it's like a bright shooting star.
As soon as the sunlight hits my window, it's like a new beginning.
As soon as the sunlight hits my window, I get a fresh feeling.
As soon as the sunlight hits my window, I can't wait to get up to a new day.

Sunlight is bright and beautiful,
Sunlight is a great feeling,
Sunlight is later overcome by night,
Sunlight is not a time to fight.

Alexandra Gordon (13)
Hillcrest School

Leaving Home

We're leaving,
Leaving home,
I dunno why,
But we are.
I'll leave Shenice,
My very best friend,
We'll leave this house,
It's been ours for long.
We'll leave my sister,
She's a sister for life.
She's at uni,
Reading medicine.
Mum and I
Equally angry,
Don't wanna leave
Our rich life behind.
We're staying put,
We're going nowhere,
But Dad is,
For all his life.
This family is gone,
This family is history.

Tolu Oyewale (13)
Hillcrest School

Christmas Is Here

Christmas is coming,
Everyone cheer,
The robins are humming,
It's drawing near!

The turkey is cooking,
The decorations are up,
Everything's festive-looking,
Egg-nog fills my cup!

The pressies are under the tree,
Wrapped in different coloured paper,
Excitement builds in me,
But I must wait till later.

We've eaten Christmas dinner,
Opened pressies too,
I wish I felt a bit thinner,
Cos I've eaten loads, that's true!

Christmas is nearly over,
But we've all had really good fun,
We all can't wait till next year,
So all can be re-done!

Natalie Tassa (12)
Hillcrest School

Winter Nightmares

Winter is coming,
The cold nights are here,
Wrap up warm for the fear again.
Don't be afraid,
Don't be scared,
Just do as he says and you'll be fine.

He's back again,
Oh look, with a smile,
What is he wearing?
My old pyjamas.
Keep calm and quiet,
Without any movements,
He'll be here again,
When it snows again.

Stacey Walters (11)
Hillcrest School

LEAVING HOME

Different thoughts in my mind.
Should I feel happy, should I feel scared,
Should I leave, should I stay?
I don't even think I'm prepared.

I might not manage leaving my home,
How will I cope?
Will my life turn out a mess?
All I have to do is hope.

Leaving my friends, leaving my school,
Changing my whole lifestyle.
Maybe I don't want to leave.
Would my life be spoilt?

All I have to do is hope and pray
That everything will be OK.
I have different feelings.
I'll never know, I might want to stay.

Deana Aldred (13)
Hillcrest School

STARS

I come out at night and brighten up the sky,
I shine very bright and even I don't know why.
When you're afraid and scared where you lie,
Just look out the window, you may see me go by.

As you're asleep, I twinkle and shine,
The sky belongs to me now,
It's mine, only mine.

When the sun rises, then I fade away,
Preparing the day for you to play.

You may not see me but I'm always there,
The sun's taken over and doesn't want to share.
As the sun goes down, then I'll reappear,
The clouds are upset and cry out a tear.

I come out at night and brighten up the sky,
I've had my rest,
It's time for yours now, goodbye!

Mikaela Reece (13)
Hillcrest School

BRITTNEY ALL ABOUT THE GHETTO

B is for better than the rest,
R is for rough and simply the best,
I is for incredible, cuz lay-D fece-t is just unbeatable,
T is for tiger, cuz when I get rough, I take you higher,
T is for tiger, cuz when I get caught, I get really hyper,
N is for nice, cuz all the cheesy gyal dem act like little mice,
E is for enjoyment, cuz you know it's all about the egg-fried rice,
Y is for Yo Yo li'l cash crew, I've got your back for true.

Brittney Mitchell (13)
Hillcrest School

BULLIED

Walking through the gates, shaking with fear,
You always know they're somewhere.

The fright inside makes you dread every turn,
The pain deep down seems to burn and burn.

One little slip, that's it, you're dead,
A kick in the stomach, a punch in the head.

Your life's not worth living, you just want to die,
The miserable days just pass by and by.

Yes, I know I'll stand up for what I believe,
I'm saved, they're expelled, oh what a relief!

I'm happier now, I have a best friend,
She says she'll stick by me, till the very end.

Chantal Watkins (12)
Hillcrest School

THE THINGS I DO

The things I do just seem to go wrong,
I remember one time I tried to make up a song,
I scratched, I racked, I went cock-a-doodle doo,
I think I sounded like a chicken, my friends did too.
The things I do just seem to get in a mess,
I remember one time I ripped my silver dress.
I was ashamed and I was blamed
But I remained being ashamed.
The things I do, I always try,
Some people think, why?
But I don't care what they think,
At least I'm doing something.

Nadine Riley (12)
Hillcrest School

Leaving Home

Why shall we move from here?
Leaving home, the last thing on Earth.
No way José, I am not moving from here.

As you leave, leaving home,
The best boyfriend you can never leave,
As you cry, he blows you a kiss,
Waving to you goodbye.

Shooting through the sky,
As you pass the moonlight,
You close your eyes as you cry,
Wishing you were near home.

Harpreet Garcha (13)
Hillcrest School

Party

I like parties, they are great,
Well, in fact, they are ace.
I also like parties when we all meet
And also when we get to eat.

Games are the best at parties,
Leaving is the worst.
The cake is also the best at parties,
Because I get to eat it first!

Now everybody is sad
Because the time has come to leave,
But we just have to think,
What great fun we have had.

Chloe Stokes (11)
Hillcrest School

SUPERMARKET SHOPPING

Apples, avocado,
Chicken, chutney,
Dough balls, doughnuts and dumplings,
Don't forget pumpkins.
Big, juicy watermelons,
Giant turkeys,
Some sour lemons
And a big chunk of cheese.
A small jar of honey, fresh from the bees.
Rosy-red apples
And furry Kiwis.
Beef mince and mushrooms
With Bolognese sauce,
Lovely green pasta
And pavlova, of course.

An awkward trolley,
Full to the top,
Can't do the lottery,
Machine's packed up.
Aisles full of people,
Clash, crash and bang,
Shelves are all empty,
Complaints fly around.
Bakery's been wiped clean,
No fresh meat in sight,
Tins are all dented,
Even the fruit on the shelves has fermented.
Queues are miles long
I'll be waiting all day,
I hate doing the shopping
And it's no different today.

Philippa Cope (12)
Hillcrest School

STAR

I am fire, sparks flying,
In the deep, dark galaxy,
Watching, waiting to die.
Others around me
Exploding, moving,
Here I am, lonely,
Watching, waiting.

Sitting in a constellation,
I make shapes in the sky,
Twinkling in the night,
My job is to keep others company,
Our roaring disturbing the still night.

And here I am, a little star,
Just waiting.

Vanessa Barlow (14)
Hillcrest School

SOUL TORN

Soul torn, tattered, lost,
Breathing, gasping, breaths of air,
Screaming into the lost sun,
Praying for the insanity to come.
Wishful sighs and empty lies
Brand me as a sideshow freak,
Left alone, disguised by tears,
I cry to hear a sound,
Wipe a tear to be touched,
Sleep to dream this all away.
The beauty of dreams, pure and simple,
Held by love in arms of purest light.

Charlotte Shough (15)
Hillcrest School

SEASONS GREETINGS

First comes spring
When all the birds sing,
Lambs are finally born
And bright green goes the lawn.
The sun comes out,
Squirrels run about,
That's what I like about springtime.

Next comes summer,
When the boys get funnier.
The flowers grow big
And the children play tig.
The holiday comes
And I meet up with my chums.
That's what I like about summertime.

Then comes fall,
When not much happens at all.
It's when school should start
And you begin to get smart,
But sometimes we have fun
After all the work we've done.
That's what I love about the fall.

Then last comes wintertime
And Christmas goes by, too quickly, but fine.
We wear warm clothes when it snows,
Because that's just the way it goes.
I almost always catch a cold,
But I don't need to be told
That it's wintertime.

Jocella Davis (12)
Hillcrest School

Summer To Winter

Green leaves,
Full trees,
Scorching heat,
Burning seats,
Lazy days,
Long summer nights,
No more school,
More than a fortnight.
No more homework
Or alarm clock's rings,
Summer gathers all these things!

Icicles cracking,
Falling snow,
Christmas coming,
Plenty to show.
Hot turkey,
Frozen ponds,
Magic wands,
Santa and Rudolph,
Ivy and holly,
'Tis the season to be jolly!

Zahra Taki (12)
Hillcrest School

My Birthday Cheers

Birthday cheers are just for you,
Shiny wrapping paper and presents too!
The happy feelings of your special day,
Nobody or nothing would dare to fray.
As they all took a deep breath to sing that joyful song,
I noticed something was finally wrong.

I dreamt of that sweet, well-decorated cake,
But I knew if there wasn't that delightful cake,
It would all clearly be fate.
As I stretched to say goodnight,
My special, decorated cake was gleaming in the moonlight,
All so perfect, shiny and round,
All night long, next door moaned,
Because of the birthday cheers that were all for me!

Lauren Thomas (14)
Hillcrest School

My Every Wish

You lock me up inside your mind,
I wait for a release.
The love you once gave made me blind,
Now it is deceased.
You stole the key to open my heart,
Then locked your own heart out.
Once so near; now far apart,
I never had a doubt.
The tears I cry don't mean a thing,
You haunt me in my dreams
Of baby breath and angel's wing,
You are behind my screams.
Eyes once so pure, now cold and dead,
Your smile has turned to dust,
I remember what a friend once said,
'It is not love, it's lust.'
If what she said is now true,
Why do I feel like this?
Every thought consumed by you,
You are my every wish.

Stacey Graham (15)
Hillcrest School

BLACK ROSE / YELLOW ROSE

Black rose woven through lilies,
Obviously not accepted in the arrangement.
Stripped of thorn and thrown in a vase,
The lilies are bought, but not you.
Petals are a soft caress, your stem firm and strong.
Slow bloomer - survivor, isolated and used to it.
Sarcasm is your defence mechanism.

Yellow rose, you pass from hand to hand.
You were plucked early for your beauty.
You bear your thorns as a warning,
Your petals are soft, your fragrance sweet upon the air.
Used to being among many and yet isolated.

Two roses, different to the eyes and yet similar.
They appreciate and complement each other,
But the hands that appreciate one, do not appreciate the other.
So they are separated for the betterment of the rose.
Each isolated again and used to it.

Sky Nash (13)
Hillcrest School

FRIENDS

I have a friend who is older than me,
She knew me before I was two or three,
She changed my nappies and smelt them too,
She even helped me lose the flu.
Before I knew it I grew,
Because my friend helped me to.
I have a friend who is older than me.
Just guess who it could be? My mom.

Danielle Brennan (12)
Hillcrest School

SUMMERTIME

It's summertime,
So have some fun,
Have a party
And drink some rum.

Go outside and enjoy the sun,
Let's all get together, it's so much fun.
Put on the music,
Start to move it,
I know you can dance, so go on, prove it.

It's so nice and hot,
Don't want to eat anything hot,
Need something cool,
I think I'd rather jump in the pool.

Well, it's summer.
Look, there's the sun,
So why not join in
And have some fun?

Nicole Thomas (12)
Hillcrest School

BIRTHDAY

Birthday, birthday,
Why do we celebrate this day?
Birthday, birthday,
Will it ever go away?
Birthday, birthday,
Why, why this day?
Birthday, birthday,
The day I celebrate my birthday.

Hannah Giles (13)
Hillcrest School

SOMETIMES

Sometimes people hurt my feelings,
Like a leaf falling off a tree in autumn.
Sometimes I feel happy,
Like a flower growing in spring.
Sometimes I'm split into two,
A part of me is happy and a part of me is sad,
Like a tree chopped in half
And the bad bits are thrown away
And the good bits are kept.

Why do I feel like this?
I don't know.
I have a loving family
And nice friends,
But sometimes we fall out,
But everyone does.

Maybe I will change some day,
But until that day,
I will feel like this sometimes.

Siobhan Lindsay Thompson (11)
Hillcrest School

CHRISTMAS IS HERE!

Christmas is here,
Hip, hip, hooray,
Get out the beer,
Let's have a great day.

I can smell the turkey,
Yum, yum, yum,
I can't wait to eat it
Cos it was cooked by my mum.

I can hear the doorbell,
My family are here,
It's only Auntie Sal
And she's bringing more beer.

Melissa Corbett (12)
Hillcrest School

My Grandma

My grandma,
She can walk quite far
But not without getting a pain in her knee
And when she does, I hear her calling me.

My grandma,
She has a mobile phone
And when it rings, she doesn't feel alone.
My grandma, she does not smoke
And that's because she's one of the old folk.

My grandma,
Her hair hasn't turned grey,
But she always says it will some day.
My grandma, she wears a bit of gold
And she's glad her skin doesn't fold.

My grandma,
She has light brown hair
And her decisions are always fair.
My grandma has light brown eyes
And she hates her grandchildren telling lies.

Tenisha Bennett (12)
Hillcrest School

It's Coming Your Way

It's a bomb waiting to go off,
5, 4, 3, 2, 1, *bang!*
Think about your family, do they sometimes let you down?
Do you feel as if you're sinking right down through the ground?
They're the only family you've got,
So thank them quite a lot.

You can't preserve your life,
But you can preserve your love.
Don't wait until they've gone, to explain about this love.
I know you love them really,
No matter what they do,
So when you're arguing with them, think about their feelings too.

When they're sick, you're by their bed,
Until it comes to the worst . . .
When you're letting them go.
Think, it's going to happen eventually,
So why not now?
It's coming to you soon,
But until then, enjoy the life you've got
And don't let your kids down.

Claire Jones (12)
Hillcrest School

Fire

I warm you on a winter's night,
I entertain you on Bonfire Night,
I can destroy a family,
I can wipe out a whole forest, overnight,
I burn high in the sky,
I can set a house alight with one single spark.

Laura Hegarty (13)
Hillcrest School

The Unwanted Presence

Every night as I get ready to go to sleep,
With fear in my heart, into bed I leap,
The dark, black room with its fearful essence
Is known to me as the Unwanted Presence.

I patiently wait for me to sink,
For then I cannot and will not blink,
Therefore erased is the dark, fearful essence
Which I call the Unwanted Presence.

Now asleep, away from the frightening stuff,
Darkness is close, but not close enough.
Forever now I am sleeping in a cheerful essence,
I no longer fear the Unwanted Presence.

Chanelle Allen (12)
Hillcrest School

Fairy Land

Welcome to Fairy Land,
Where your dreams will all come true,
Where fairies play hopscotch
All day long, up and down the lane.

Baby fairies trying to fly before they crawl,
Father fairies chuffed to the max
Because their wives have given birth
To beautiful baby fairies.

Welcome to the fairy town.
This is where you get the train.
Goodbye, so long,
I hope you had a good time in Fairy Land.

Fayola Morris (12)
Hillcrest School

CELEBRATIONS

C elebrations are memorable, whether they're good or bad.
E very celebration holds something special.
L istening to stories from the past . . . some are really sad.
E verybody sitting, all relaxed.
B irthdays, Christmas, anniversaries, Easter - they're all special celebrations to me.
R eligious or non-religious, who cares what they are? It's just an excuse to celebrate.
A unties, uncles, cousins, neighbours, grandma, you name them, they're all here?
T omorrow, it'll be over, we'd better make it worthwhile.
I don't want it to be over, the atmosphere's just right.
O h well, I'll just have to wait till next year now.
N ever mind, we still had fun and we will remember it again next year.
S oon it'll be here again and the countdown's just started!

Natasha Ubhoo (14)
Hillcrest School

THE SUN

The sun, hot and shining,
The sun shines like a golden crown.
The sun glows like a golden queen.
The sun waves her beautiful hands,
The sun is yellower than the yoke of an egg.
The sun makes the world feel bright.
The sun is as bright as a glass of orange juice.
The sun shines like a golden goddess.
The sun, the queen of brightness.
The sun gives everyone the idea of a summer holiday.
The sun, the nation's lover.

Vivian Ezugha (11)
Hillcrest School

Birthday Special!

Your birthday is something to look forward to,
But what if it is on Hallowe'en?
Just think of the fun and excitement,
You could go trick or treating,
You could go to a shopping mall and spend your money.
If you were at school, you'd get presents from your friends,
But when you went home and found out there was a large present,
What would you do?
Would you stare at it?
Would you open it?
You don't know.
You decide to open it,
'Happy Birthday!'
Someone or something shouted.
You ran out of the door and didn't want to come back.
Ha, ha, ha!

Dinah Osborne (12)
Hillcrest School

Rain

I flood the street with puddles,
I soak people's clothes until they are dripping,
I wet people's windscreens so they can't see where they're going,
I am the one who put up the umbrellas.
I like to see dogs' fur get messy,
I'm the one who sees the people run inside.
I flood rivers and flow into the sea.
I like people's food to get sloppy,
I feed the plants to make them grow.
When I come out, the kids to away.

Veneita Belnavis (13)
Hillcrest School

FRIENDS!

Friends, who needs them?
Not me, no not me,
All they do is hurt me,
Punch me and call me names.
That's why I'm here today,
On the roof.

They have driven me here,
No one likes me.
Why was I created?
Shall I jump?
Bye . . .

My hair is flying through the air, I am free.
Am I dead? I can't be,
I see blue, the sky.
I see someone, who is it?
Oh, it's you!

Claire Kennedy (12)
Hillcrest School

SUNLIGHT

I am the one who stands
Out in the world.
I shine,
I bring warmth
To the whole Earth.
I make people hot,
I bring light,
I am the source of light,
I am the sunlight.

Harpreet Dhariwal (13)
Hillcrest School

A Girl Called Sam

There was a young girl called Sam,
Who had a nice young man.
She stayed at his house
And saw a big mouse
Which frightened young Sam away.

The man went running after young Sam,
But fell into a baby's pram.
He cut open his head
And got rushed to a bed
And Sam looked like she was nearly dead.

Sam went running to the man
To give him a sandwich of ham.
She told him she loved him
And he said he loved her
And they were happy together forever.

Emma White (14)
Hillcrest School

Love And Separation

I am love,
I fill people's hearts with joy,
I make people happy,
I am Cupid in disguise,
I am the things you feel inside.

I am separation,
I make people sad,
I destroy relationships,
I am bad.

Yeji Im (13)
Hillcrest School

THE RAINBOW

The rainbow is so pretty,
It's colourful and bright,
When people look at it they say,
'Oh, what a pretty sight.'
It's caused when rain and sunshine clash,
And if you can find the end you could find some cash.
The rainbow is red, yellow, green and blue too,
So here's a song, just for you:
'Red and yellow and pink and green,
Orange and purple and blue,
I can sing a rainbow,
Sing a rainbow,
Sing a rainbow too.'
You probably know the song from when you were younger,
I hope you can keep this in your head even longer.
God made the sight for us,
So when you look at it, remember Him!

Sophie Martin (12)
Hillcrest School

THE GRIM REAPER

Hallowe'en, All Hallows Eve,
You only believe what you believe.
A time for remembering all of the dead,
Things they have done and things they have said.
The dark Grim Reaper, is going to come,
When your life is over, dead and done.
His cloaked hand, or is it a claw?
Reaches out for your life in an orb.
He takes it and you drop to the floor,
Then everyone knows that you are no more.

Emily Bailey (12)
Hillcrest School

WAR

The men set off in rows of four,
Their suits done up and guns in place
And they sing a song of fighting.
    'We take no prisoners,
    We show no mercy,
    We are the army
    And we are ready for war.'
They get to the battlefield,
Their shields are up,
Their guns are full,
It's time for war.
    'We take no prisoners,
    We show no mercy,
    We are the army,
    And we are ready for war.'

Natasha Buchanan (12)
Hillcrest School

FRIDAY

Friday's here,
Discoing's near,
Go out with all my friends
And have a few beers!
Stay up late
With my best mate,
Telling stories and desires,
Watching films with Mike Myers.
Having a laugh,
Chillin' in the bath,
Waiting and wishing for another night of wrath.

Fatima Taki (12)
Hillcrest School

CHRISTMAS

Christmas is a time for sharing,
Christmas is a time for caring.
The lights sparkle upon the tree,
The family celebrate, including me.
The turkey in the oven cooks slow,
While the coals in the fire glow.
The snow is falling on the ground
As Santa Claus flies all around.
The parties all start to swing,
'Hooray for Christmas,' we all sing.

Rachael Dyson (11)
Hillcrest School

THE SUN AND THE STARS

I awake from my sleep to find that big fireball in the sky
And finally when I get to school,
It gleams through the window, watching and waiting.
When day is done, he'll be there,
That big fireball in the air,
But night peeks round the corner,
The stars light up the darkest skies
And I know they'll stay all night!

Angela Evans (11)
Hillcrest School

VALENTINE'S DAY

Imagine a scene on Valentine's Day,
With a couple sitting in the front room,
With roses and chocs placed on the table
And a dinner and wine on there too.

You hear the sound of them laughing loudly,
Kissing on a piece of spaghetti,
On Valentine's Day we think of love
And hearts and flowers - don't forget me!

Felicity Brennan (12)
Hillcrest School

ALL ABOUT FRUITS

Melon is so sweet,
It's good enough to eat.
I really don't like a pear,
Because it makes me swear.
I kind of like a peach,
It reminds me of the beach.
I always eat my mango,
So I can jump and tango.
Different fruits are everywhere,
Except when you go to the fair.

Nyoka McKenzie (12)
Hillcrest School

HALLOWE'EN

Hallowe'en is a night to be seen,
It is where the children stay up all night,
Where they scare and have a fright.
People always gather in the street
And say the magic words, 'Trick or treat?'
Knocking on the doors with their bags of sweets,
Saying, 'Can we have something nice to eat?'

Cherrelle Francis-Smith (13)
Hillcrest School

WEEPING WILLOW

Weeping willow why do you cry?
At night you seem your worst,
You howl like the wind,
Creak like a gate
And sway with the river's current.
Yet during the day,
You are so quiet,
Your head hung low,
Branches drooped as though you were reaching for underworld spirits.
People walk by and ignore your crying,
Though they could not hear it.
Only if you stand right up close,
Can you hear your little sobs.
So weeping willow why do you cry?
Please tell me weeping willow,
With all your beauty and splendour,
What reason have you to cry?
Please tell me weeping willow,
Why do you cry?

Abigail Coward (14)
James Brindley School

TWO FACES

Beyond all life
From misery and pain
Life of all
People laughing
Smiley and happy

Different ways
Way of the eternal
Way of my heart
Two faces.

Westley Yates (15)
James Brindley School

BULLIES

They make fun of me
They take the mick
They're always there
To give me stick
I can't escape
There's nowhere to go
They make me feel sad
They make me feel low
Why do they hate me?
What have I done?
They're round every corner
There's nowhere to run
They whisper and nudge each other
They giggle and stare
There must be something wrong with me
But why me? It's not fair!
They're loud and they're sarky
They're nasty and rude
I never touch them
So what's with the bad attitude?

Melanie Brown (15)
James Brindley School

TOBY'S LIFE

When I'm upset or in fear,
Toby my dog will always be here.
He will play with his toy bone,
When we go out he's all alone.
He does cope well,
But then sometimes he is the dog from Hell!
If he does something stupid,
He then acts like a cupid.
With his dark brown puppy-dog eyes,
He puts himself on the floor and dies.
In the garden he chases the birds until they fly away,
When he's done you can tell, he smiles and is gay.
Toby protects us from strangers,
Warns us all of the dangers.
When the geese are mean,
Toby thinks they're obscene.
He enters the park,
And runs like a spark.
Toby sniffs the grass,
And loves a particular lass.
Martha is her name,
Toby thinks there's no one the same.
He is very gentle and soft to touch,
I love Toby very much.
He's a babe in my heart,
When he passes, it will be difficult to part.

Suzanne Bralee (13)
James Brindley School

FALL OUT

(Based on 'Fall In' by Harold Begbie)

What will you lack sonny, what will you lack
If you never come back?
Girls drowning their sorrows for the lads that have perished
For the lovers they've lost, and the ones they have cherished
Will you end a strangled cheer to the sky
Or will you come back with only one eye?

Where will you look sonny, where will you look
When you're cornered by guns and spears?
When your wife's got no husband, and your children no dad
Do you really want to give them a life that's so bad?
Will you say it was naught to you in France
But then get only one last glance?

How will you fare sonny, how will you fare
When you lie freezing cold and you're breathing no air?
Will you fall and die tomorrow?
Will you let your wife drown her sorrows
Or will you stay with your wife and child
And live to see a future, calm and mild?

Why do they call sonny, why do they call?
Do they want you to risk your life and slowly fall?
Your wife and children need you more than they
So why don't you just be safe and stay?
What will you do sonny, what will you do
When your family and friends are burying you?

Gemma Cullen (13)
Shenley Court School

World Peace

If I could I would
Change the world for good
I'd go to countries and knock on doors
I'd put a stop to all the wars.

I dream of helping the old and needy
Share our food, let's not be greedy
I'd give a little of what I've got
Sometimes it doesn't take a lot.

Let's love one another
Treat me as your brother
Put a stop to all the fighting
I'd like that to be in writing.

At the end of the day
I'll get my way
It'll take a long time
For a world without crime.

I'll spread the word
And if you haven't heard
Love is the way
To a brand new day.

Sean Gibbs (13)
Shenley Court School

Poem

Should we go to school today,
Go to lessons, eat and play?
On sponsors day we need to run,
Or shall we just sit and have fun?

Or should we wag school today,
Run around town and play all day?
And we could rob some sweets,
Oh, this is a real treat.

Rachel Guttridge (13)
Shenley Court School

THE WAR SOUNDS!

Fighting his way through the clouds
In battle formation, watched by the crowds
He drops the bomb, it plunges to the ground
Making an awful, deafening sound
Planes darting through the mists
Taking an awful amount of risks
Bren guns blazing
Air forces amazing
He draws into the hanger
And victory starts off, with a banger!

Rebekah Moles (13)
Shenley Court School

MY DREAM

One night I went to bed,
With these funny dreams in my head.
They were about this monster,
That tried to knock me dead.
I kept running
And the monster kept coming.
And that was the end of my dream in bed!

Kenneth Bedder (12)
Shenley Court School

FALL OUT

(Based on 'Fall In' by Harold Begbie)

What will you lack sonny, what will you lack
When you never come back?
Shouting their love to long-lost lads
Or coming back they end up going mad
What will you lack, when your mate goes by
With a girl who will never see his smile?

Where will you go sonny, where will you hide
When bullets come shooting by?
You can't find your girls anywhere to hide
Leaving your lady you love and cherish
Your children left questioning, where is my daddy?
When do you tell them he's never coming back?

How will you look sonny, how will you care
When you just have to stare?
When they sit by the fire in your old chair
But you're all the way up there
When they got their own family, they shall not care.

Why do they call God, why do they call
For me or men all brave and strong
When is it their turn when and why?
Was it rightful to be forced by a war?
When will I see them again
That's what you'll lack sonny, that's what you'll lack.

Jacqueline Caulkin (13)
Shenley Court School

Fall Out

(Based on 'Fall In' by Harold Begbie)

What will you lack sonny, what will you lack
If you never come back?
No one will be waiting for you
Silence for when the lads come back
From the foe they rushed from the beat
There will be silence when you come back
Cry till your eyes turn red

Where will you look sonny, where will you look
Sonny with no arms or legs?
Your children on their own wanting their dad
But where will you look when they give you a glance
And say what happened to him
Then what will you say when they ask?

How will you fare sonny, how will you fare?
If you're not aware
In the cold winter night
When you're in your coffin or a wheelchair
And say what have I done to deserve this
I wish I never went, why did I go?

Why do they call sonny, why do they call
For men who are weak and foolish?
When your brothers are fine, just cut and bruised
And you with no arms or legs.

Matt Simpson (13)
Shenley Court School

Fall Out!

(Based on 'Fall In' by Harold Begbie)

What will you lack sonny, what will you lack
If you're treated like a stranger?
Nobody cares for you, so watch your back!
You expect to *die* in the danger
Nobody will care if you get blown up
Only your precious family
Never again, no never
Will they live completely happy?

Where will you look sonny, where will you look
When your children are fatherless?
Look at them, think of them, how would you feel?
Their life would be a muddled up mess
If you went away and never came home
Imagine what life would be like
They'd feel strange without you, they'd be all alone
No father for the new baby, the little tyke!

How will you fare sonny, how will you fare
When you sleep, freezing cold in a trench?
Wouldn't you rather live life without care
And doze on a sunny park bench?
I hope you can stand all that freezing cold weather
It will drive you round the bend
You'll be sitting there at the end of your tether
Has anyone got a coat to lend?

Why do they call sonny, why do they call
For you, when you could stay at home?
It's better to be there, it's not good to fall
In the war you will not be known!
Whilst you're sitting in the snow
Wishing, wanting, waiting
Thinking what you'll have to show
Bravery, fearlessness, daring.

Sarah Pipe (13)
Shenley Court School

Who Am I?

I wonder who I am?
I'm not very sure,
Maybe I'm born to help people,
Maybe I'm born to be nasty to people,
Or maybe I'm born to be myself, to see how I end up.

I wonder who I am?
Am I tall or short,
Am I fat or thin,
Who knows, it's early days.

I wonder who I am?
I wasn't very sure,
I'm still not sure,
But it's becoming clearer and clearer each day . . . and every day.

I was born for a reason soon that reason will be clear,
I grow every day into who I am,
Who am I? . . . me and that's all that matters.

Luke Noble (12)
Shenley Court School

Fall Out

(Based on 'Fall In' by Harold Begbie)

What will you lack sonny, what will you lack
If you never come back?
Screaming girls line up in the street
Screaming their love when you never meet
Will you send a letter of goodbye
When you go to Heaven in the sky?
What will you lack when the girl goes by
With the man that made you die?

Where will you look sonny, where will you look
When you know your children are crying
Over knowing your children have no dad
In the war that destroyed many men?
Will you say it was just meant to be
Even though he hurt you and me?
But where will you look when you get the chance
When you know your life has passed?

How will you bare sonny, how will you bare
In the cold winter nights
When you could be sitting by the fire in your old man's chair
And listening to stories told by the mayor
Of how the war was bad and sad
And people have died from going mad?
But *no,* you had to go there and not have a care
Say, oh please say, I was not one to go.

Why do they call sonny, why do they call
For men that are silly and daft
Who are willing to give up just like that
When you could be at a picture show
Or down the pub or betting the odds?
But you had to fight in the war
Now your family cry as you have died
Because you had to fight in the war.

Gemma Broad (13)
Shenley Court School

Fall Out

(Based on 'Fall In' by Harold Begbie)

What will you lack sonny, what will you lack?
Going to war, what for?
Seeing all the horrible sights, no torches, no candles, no lights
Crying every night, under the moonlight
Wishing you were home rather than alone, what for?

When will you look sonny, when will you look?
With your whole life ahead of you
Instead of thinking about what you are going to do
Fighting for your country, what for?

How will you fare sonny, how will you fare?
Attacking people for no reason
Just for your country, what for?

Why do they call sonny, why do they call?
What for sonny, is it the law?
I hope you've thought about what I've written
So take the right road and not the wrong road, think about it!

Chervorne Jeffers (13)
Shenley Court School

Fall Out

(Based on 'Fall In' by Harold Begbie)

What will you lack sonny, what will you lack?
When you go to the same grey sky and love for God seems to die.
Terrified of the memories of blood and gore
Just stay at home, safe behind the door.

Where will you look sonny, where will you look?
Rattling rifles fill the sky
You haven't a chance, you're bound to die
You die for your country, they killed you for fun
The memories have already gone.

How will you fare sonny, how will you fare?
They know where you are, they're coming for you
They'll kill you and your army too
They blew you off the face of the Earth
The memories come back from when your mother gave birth.

Why do they call sonny, why do they call?
People go to war to be big and brave
The government uses them for a war slave
It doesn't matter if you win
Another war's about to begin.

James McGuire (13)
Shenley Court School

My Dream Of A Better Place

If I would I could stop all war
If I would I could end poverty for sure
If I would I could cure all illness
If I would I could create a ray of happiness
I have a dream of healthy people.

Luke Alan Dudley (13)
Shenley Court School

FALL OUT

(Based on 'Fall In' by Harold Begbie)

What will you lack sonny, what will you lack?
When you don't come back
When your family is weeping
And you're in deep sleeping

What will you do sonny, what will you do?
When you haven't a clue
When your children are sad
Because they have no dad

What will you gain sonny, what will you gain?
When blood poured like rain
You shot someone when you were dared
And now you're dead, no one cared

What will you lose sonny, what will you lose?
When you're all over the news
He'll never see his family again
Both his sons who were ten.

Marty Hales (13)
Shenley Court School

WHO DO I WANT TO BE LIKE?

I want to be like Spider-man so I can walk on walls,
I want to be like a daredevil so I can do what I want,
I want to be like Bat Girl so I can fly in the sky,
I want to be like Superman so I have super-strength,
I want to be like a penguin so I can stand the cold,
I want to be like Iron Man so I am made of iron,
Now I think about it I don't want to be like any of these
I just want to be me.

Daniel Allinson (11)
Shenley Court School

WHO AM I?

Who am I?
I am me
I am known by God
Who made me so

Who am I?
I am a creation
Who am I?
Because he made me so

Why am I here?
To work for Jesus
To learn about him
To teach about his love

Who am I?
I am me
Why am I me?
Because I can shout
I can shout about his love

Why am I here?
To pray
To worship
To live with him
And for him to live with me

Who am I?
I am me
That's who I am.

Lisa Bick (14)
Shenley Court School

Fall Out

(Based on 'Fall In' by Harold Begbie)

What will you lack sonny
What will you lack?
When all your mates die
And you never said bye
When you see horrible sights
All because of fights.

Where will you look sonny
Where will you look?
When you see your own blood
All in the mud
When you're half-dead
In a hospital bed
Where will you look?

How will you fare sonny
How will you fare?
When your kids are at home
All alone
And where's Daddy?
Mom's saying he's a baddie.

Why do they call sonny, why do they call?
When you're at war
And they come to your door
When they shoot you
What can you do
When you're dead
And your kids sit beside your bed
Why do they call?

Sarah Clarke (14)
Shenley Court School

I Have A Dream

I have a dream where nobody dreams
Instead they make things happen for themselves
The world would be a better place
If only things were done
Not just dreamt
Like war, everyone dreams about no more wars
But then again that's just a dream
If only someone would do something about it
Get up and tell the world.
Stop.
Think
And listen!
Greenpeace save the environment
Don't litter.
Don't do this
Don't do that.
We need to start somewhere
Maybe we should listen to ourselves
Dream of helping never quite doing it
We are living in a dreamer's world.
What's your dream?

Emma-Jean Craig (14)
Shenley Court School

Poem

Do those dreams you dream fade away?
Do those dreams you dream ever come back?
Do you ever wish those dreams would come true?
Do your parents make fun of you when you tell them your dreams?
Does anyone think that you care about your country in your sleep?
Does anyone know your ambitions?

Emma Owen (13)
Shenley Court School

For King And Country?

All the young men keen to join up -
Hurrying to the trenches, but what for?
Trenches are dirty, muddy,
Like open graves with rats scurrying between
The arms and legs of the brave young men.
Who would want to be a part of this carnage?

Screaming bombs like out of control fireworks,
Chase the stars away in the dark night sky.
Is this hell on Earth like we've never known before?

Is king and country worth the fight
When loved ones don't come back?
Those that do are broken men
Possessed by the demon of evil.
Crippled bodies
Devoured by wild green mustard gas,
The silent, spreading killer.

The medals,
The honour,
The glory
Cannot bring back a life.

Eleanor Hewitt (14)
Shenley Court School

My Mom

P lay with your little sister Mark
O h Mom, I was going to the park
E very day you go there.
M om, stop moaning all the while.
S hut up boy, run a mile.

Wesley Swadkins (11)
Shenley Court School

My Day At The Zoo

I went to the zoo
And saw a gnu
I went a bit further
And saw a pink panther
I was very perky until
I saw a turkey.
I saw a cat eat a rat.
I went to stroke a goat
But it jumped on a boat.
So when I went further
It began to rain
And the drains were flooded
It stopped raining and everything was damp,
The shops were dripping
From the drain pipes
We had to go under the shelter
To keep ourselves dry
And I had to take my trainers off
And put my wellingtons on
But it was a good day in the end.

Stacey Geoghan (11)
Shenley Court School

My Nonsense Poem

If you've got a big baboon
You could take it to a lagoon.
If you have a stinking rat
You can swap it for a cat.
Can you get a great big turkey
Put it in the sea all murky.
Horses can be pretty big
Make sure it doesn't start to dig.

Tiger lurks in the bush,
Waiting for someone to rush.
The scary bear
Just might care.
If you have a gorgeous deer
You can get a good career.
To get rid of a silly mug,
Go and get a big good dog.

Kay Wilson (11)
Shenley Court School

What Lacks
(Based on 'Fall In' by Harold Begbie)

What would you lack sonny, what would you lack
if you don't come back you would be kept in a sack
and people treading on your back.

Kids are crying while fathers are dying
in the trench low in stench
realising your mates are dead
and bombs are blowing legs off men.

Mean boys are flying and dying
while people are crying and sighing
people are injured and dying,
medics are flying to see the dying.

Bombs are dropping while heads are flopping
bullets are firing while people are freezing
while old men are wheezing
and people are sneezing
is it worth it, is it worth it?

Gary O'Toole (13)
Shenley Court School

Fall Out

(Based on 'Fall In' by Harold Begbie)

What will you lack sonny, what will you lack,
Your loving family, your life?
What will you gain sonny, what will you gain,
The fear on the end of the knife?

Where will you look sonny, where will you look,
When the others look down as you pass?
Where will you go sonny, where will you go,
When you are one of the last?

How will you fare sonny, how will you fare,
When you look at the stars above?
What will you care sonny, what will you care,
When you have no women to love?

Why do they call sonny, why do they call,
What do they want you to fight for?
Tell yourself this sonny, tell yourself this,
You're worthless if you go to war.

Emma Lee (14)
Shenley Court School

The Sound Of Silence In The Classroom

It was so quiet in the classroom, all I could hear
Was the sound of the computers humming altogether,
The table creaking when people moved around it,
The bell to signal the halfway point of the lesson,
Someone clicking their pen on and off,
Someone else's pen drop on the desktop,
The traffic from outside on the road going by on their journey
And lastly someone mumbling about something.

Ruth Bennett (15)
Shenley Court School

The Last Fighting Day

Walking, trudging in this land of mud,
Explosions, guns, *thud, thud, thud.*
Crawling, wriggling, lice everywhere,
Too tired to itch, too tired to care.

Head falling forward, tears running down,
This war, this chaos, no peace to be found.
If only they'd worry, if only they'd care,
Of the screams of the innocent, of the unfair.

Bombshell falling, rolling along the ground,
Eyes lit with shock and fear of the sound.
The bang so loud, so sudden, so quick,
The damage that's done won't be easy to fix.

My head on the floor, the blood trickling down,
Slowly finding its way to the ground.
As I wait for the light to take me away,
I realise this is the last fighting day.

Samantha Webb (13)
Shenley Court School

As War Comes Closer

As the war approaches
and the days get longer
soldiers die
and people become frightened,
the crashing and banging of guns at night,
people are frightened about what will happen,
all the dead soldiers go to Heaven.

Richard Wright (13)
Shenley Court School

Fall Out

(Based on 'Fall In' by Harold Begbie)

What will you lack sonny, what will you lack
When your friends are gone and you're all alone?
All you hear are the sounds of the deadly bullets
Shooting out, *bang! Bang!*
The blood, the gore, all you see is death.
The friends you had are no more,
The relationships you had are no more.
A missing leg, a missing arm,
Is that what you want sonny?

Where will you look sonny, where will you look
When you're all alone and your friends are gone?
All you see is your friends dying and dying over and over again.
All you want is to go home, is that what you want?
Wondering if your family's there, but if not, do you really care?

How will you fare sonny, how will you fare
When you're going insane, and you can't sort it out?
In the cold winter nights nobody's there sonny.
How will you fare?
Wondering how your children are, are they missing you
Or aren't they even there?

Why do you call sonny, why do you call?
You're weak with not a care in the world.
What do you do sonny, what do you do?
What is the need, do you think
People will respect old war heroes
But what if you don't come home,
How do you think your family would feel?

Dale Feerick (13)
Shenley Court School

Fall Out

(Based on 'Fall In' by Harold Begbie)

What will you lack sonny, what will you lack
If you don't come back?
When your wife is sad
Because her child has no dad
When you son is crying
Because his dad is dying.

Where will look sonny, where will you look?
When you find you've took
The long road to disaster
You hear the cries of your master
As he lies in his trench
Nearly dead.

How will you fare sonny, how will you fare?
When you think you've been unjust
To the prisoners you've captured
And the family you share.

Why do they call sonny, why do they call?
For you out of all the world
Your son is still crying
Because he thinks you're still dying.

As the rain pours, all you can see
Are dead bodies, all around
You think to yourself
Why me sonny, why me?

Robert Faville (14)
Shenley Court School

The Art Of War

You could taste the fear in the air
As full-grown men were getting scared
Anxious to pull the trigger
But the enemy might do it quicker
Turrets aiming high
Planes ready to fly
Darkness all around
Tension on the ground
The first trigger then is pulled
And the deadly deeds are fulfilled
Murder, death everywhere
On the ground and in the air
Heartbeats stop
Corpses rot
Then the war is over.

David Smith (14)
Shenley Court School

Who Am I?

I am an old man
I am a teacher
I am a rapper
I am an English teacher
I have grey hair
I have a strange nose
I am 18, so he says.

Who am I?
Mr Miller!

Ben Robinson (12)
Shenley Court School

My Name

M y name is Mat
A nd I wear a hat
T he doormat looks like a cat
T hat people wipe their feet on
H e gets so dirty
E ven when it rains
W e are so good at poems.

H e is a good poet
I t even rhymes
N ever when you speak fast
E ven when you say it slow
S o have a good day OK.

Matthew Hines (12)
Shenley Court School

Fire, Fire!

I stand and watch,
The tree falls towards me,
With crackling sounds,
Fire passes to another
And one by one
They fall to the ground.

The sky fills with smoke,
All trees turn to ash,
I do nothing,
But stand and stare
And watch everything go
In a flash.

Sarah Ensor (14)
Shenley Court School

I Want To Be

I want to be like Superman,
Saving all the locals.

I want to be like Spider-man,
Crawling up the walls.

I want to be like a daredevil,
Playing with his life.

I want to be like Joker,
As naughty as can be.

I want to be like Flash Gordon,
Who is faster than me.

I cannot be myself
Which is hardest for me.

David Clarke (11)
Shenley Court School

If I Was

If I was an animal
I'd be a monkey
Because I am funky

If I was a bird
I'd be a hawk
To be able to hunt for prey

If I was a car
I'd be the Honda MX5
Because they are fast.

Christopher Sandford (12)
Shenley Court School

I Had A Dream

I had a dream
Peaceful, calm and cool,
If all this was the world
Everyone would be happy.

I had a dream
Everything is quiet now,
Children and adults alike,
Getting on together.

I had a dream
No war or evil,
Violence, death or deceit,
Everybody loves and cares.

Danielle Embley (13)
Shenley Court School

I Have A Dream

If I could hold the world in my hand
I would make it a crime-free land
Where all sorts of races would work together
People at peace forever and ever
Where homeless people would have a home
And orphaned children wouldn't be alone

Where all of the trees would be left to grow high
And people with chainsaws would carry on by
Where all of the animals were left to roam free
And all of the fishes could play in the sea
I have a dream, I hope it comes true
Everyone has dreams, how about you?

Emma Collins (14)
Shenley Court School

My Family Means To Me

My family means to me,
A lot of things, they are my flesh and blood,
My soul, I love them with all my heart.
My mom, the leader of the house,
My brother, my hero,
My sisters, well are just my sisters,
I can talk to my family, tell them secrets,
My family listen to me when I am feeling blue,
This is what my family are;

My mom is a flower,
My brother is a tiger,
And
My two sisters would be butterflies,
As light as feathers.

Sarah Ryan (13)
Shenley Court School

The Seventh Day

The world is made, God's work is done,
He's made the Earth, the moon and sun.
He's made the planets - Venus and Mars,
He waits for the future - electric and cars,
He's made the creatures, birds and fish,
He's acted out His childhood wish,
He's made the cosmos, planets and all,
He's made all creatures, great and small,
A whole week's work is quite enough,
He needs His rest, for this job is too tough.

Sam Connolly (13)
Shenley Court School

War Poetry

Will he bomb the world?
Can we trust this man?
Is it OK that a young family can die?
Will they then be bombed by the FBI?

Can we play through the war?
Can we play when babies' heads get blown off, I asked what for?
Then I realised it 'ent my fault
We have to just carry on regardless cos it 'ent my fault.

Will they strike again?
Will they plan it in their den?
Which weapons will they use?
And will it be big news?

Can we play through the war?
What if we get bombed whilst playin'
Then we'll be sayin'
We shouldn't have played throughout this war!

Will they bombard us?
Kill innocent civilians?
The number of deaths would be trillions,
Or would there just be a big fuss?

So, ask yourself,
Is war worth all of this?

Luke Brown (13)
Shenley Court School

Blues

My favourite footie team is the Blues
They never seem to lose.
They score so many goals
Because of their high-spirited souls.
Devlin crosses in the ball
And it ends in a bloody brawl.
Damien Johnson blows down the wing
And the crowd start to sing.
Clinton Morrison goes to score
The crowd seem to cheer more and more.
The ref blows for a pen
The opposing player runs around like a hen.
The ref tells him not to dive
The player replies, 'I'm not trying to skive.'
The blues are the Midlands' hosts
They seem to whack the Villa players' heads off the posts.

Matthew Matthews (11)
Stockland Green School

School

I like a lot of things about my school,
Even though it ain't got a swimming pool,
Or a widescreen telly,
At least the food fills up my belly.

I like a lot of things about my school,
Some of the teachers are really tall,
Some of the work is not that hard,
One or two children get in a bad mood.

I like a lot of things about my school,
Walking through the long halls,
Mr Dickson, Mr Clarke and Mrs Wood,
All the teachers are really good.

Hayley Taylor (11)
Stockland Green School

Homework

Homework, you have loads of it
Some people think it's the pits
When I do my homework I need to sit
When my homework is hard I never quit
I get out my homework when I get through the gate
Homework is sometimes great
When I've got homework I don't go out with mates
Homework is a lot of weight
Homework is not better than all the rest
Homework is not the best
It's sometimes a pest
The homework you have is sometimes a test
You don't get homework every day
You should get some pay
Where there's homework there is a way
If I don't know what to do I say
When I've finished I've got loads of time
I can do whatever I want, like a mime.
My writing is always the same
I think homework is a tiny bit lame
In primary school we hardly had any
I can't go out because I haven't got a penny
In one lot of homework we had to write about a friend,
I wrote about Danny.

Michelle Smith (12)
Stockland Green School

Wicked Witches' Brew

W itches' brew all gruesome green
I n there everything totally opposite to clean
C ackle it goes all day long
K ittens' eyeballs don't half pong!
E verything is all so *yuk!*
D ays all the same for witches.

W itches' cloaks all down to the ground
I wish I was a witch!
T all hats all billowing black.
C auldrons in the cupboards
H ooks with cloaks on
E verywhere is all so dirty
S melly socks in potions, *yuk!*

B roomsticks in the corners
R evolting things on shelves
E ar wax in one.
W itches are revolting things!

Kayleigh Gallier (12)
Stockland Green School

The Ways Of Life

Life is about you and choices
If they have been bad or good
No matter what you have or have not done
Set your sights high and you have already won

Stop thinking about yourself and think of others
Think about your friends and family
Your sisters and your brothers
Your first step in life was when you were born
Think about that day and morn

Treat life as a friend
Be kind and it'll be kind back
Be enthusiastic, show no sign of slack
Try your hardest and you will succeed
It does not matter about your past or your creed
Set your sights high and you have already won.

John Leachman (14)
Stockland Green School

THE QUEEN'S JUBILEE

The Queen's getting ready,
The Queen's having fun,
The Queen's so happy
Her Jubilee's begun.

She puts on her dress,
She puts on her shoes,
She knows she's the best,
She's not going to lose.

She walks out of her palace
Waving her hands,
She looks at everyone
Especially her fans.

She looks at her sons
And the army holding guns.
She knows she's won
And she is having fun.

She gets in a car,
She knows she's going far.
She looks at the sky
And thinks, am I a star?

Kayleigh Mason (11)
Stockland Green School

WINTER DAYS

The stars are shining
The moon is glowing
The clouds look as if
They have a silver lining.

The tree leaves are nice and crisp
The leaves are golden brown.
I hate the night, it doesn't feel right
It makes me want to frown.

The thunder and lightning
Banging and crashing.
I really hate it
It's so frightening.

Snowdrops falling from the sky
I wish the weather could be dry!
Walking in the snow
The sun looks as if it has a special glow.

Jasveer Panesar (13)
Stockland Green School

MY HOUSE

Everyone is dashing about,
I'm asking if I can go out.
School's tomorrow, there's plenty of sorrow.
Now I will go out to play
While making the most of my day.

My bedroom is in a horrible state,
My friend called ages ago, can't be late!
My little brother is in my room,
At night I'm in, he's staring at the room,
In the morning I'm up and ready whilst I sleep with my teddy.

Everyone is dashing about,
I'm asking Mum if I can go out.
School's tomorrow, there's plenty of sorrow.
Now I will go out to play,
While making the most of my day.

Jessica Dunne (11)
Stockland Green School

FIRE

Strong, powerful, blazing fire
Climbs up buildings like a cat up a tree
Some people think you're a powerful liar
You're strong, you push anything out of the way
Eating anything in your path

You have scared many
Red, yellow, orange and blue
Strong, bold colour, like your attitude
But some people like your flames

You cause lots of pennies
And lots of pain
Like I said before, people like you, but who?
Going across the world like latitude

Finally, you calm down
Hopefully never to burn again
But that is just a dream
Have a nice sleep tonight
And warm somebody tomorrow

As you wake up your head is spinning
Come on you have work to do
You race to work warming people up.

Samantha Kay (11)
Stockland Green School

The Sky

I look at the sky
And think of art,
Because it's so perfect
I think, when did they start?
It was one night in Menorca
When I saw a shooting star,
How did they do art like that
With a moving car?
Just look at the moon
In the middle of the sky,
How did Neil Armstrong get to walk on it
And why?
The Earth is our planet
But there are eight more,
Mars, Pluto, Saturn and Neptune
Can you name the other four?
As the night is over
And the day begins to dawn,
With the sun over the horizon
A brand new day is born.
The dawn chorus has started
There's a lovely blue sky,
Where white clouds go drifting
Like great ships floating by.
Evening is coming
Blue sky out of sight,
Black sky, stars again
Goodnight.

Lauren McNair (11)
Stockland Green School

SCHOOL

My school is Stockland Green
The best place I've ever been
When the bell rings we go to our lesson,
Then we jump up to another session.

They've got the best dinners,
They're just great
They're the best things
I've ever ate.

At home time,
I go to the shop,
To get some sweets
And a bottle of pop.

The day is finished
What a shame,
After all,
School isn't so lame.

I like English,
My favourite lesson.
At Stockland Green
There's no depression.

People are nice,
People are kind,
We put new things
Into our minds.

Kirsty Fitzroy (11)
Stockland Green School

OH WHAT A DAY!

Oh what a day!
What a day it was when you passed away,
You only passed away,
So why did I feel that way?
How did it feel to have your life slip through your hands?
What was it like to start your spirit's journey into the heavenly lands?
It's a wonder how you stayed on,
Stayed on until the end,
You waited until that final moment to disperse and transcend,
Your life was like a star,
It shone so bright each day,
Whenever we needed a guiding light,
We'd look up to you and admire your might,
Oh what a worthy sight!
How your words of wisdom were always right,
That's why I longed to reach up high and catch your fallen stardust,
To have your precious memories in my palm
like glowing crystals was a must,
But no longer do I feel that way,
Feel that way because,
Like the shining star you are,
I know you're watching over us.

Alexia Farrell (14)
Stockland Green School

WAR, WHAT IS IT GOOD FOR?

War, what is it good for?
Nothing!
For it brings hatred to the world.

War, what is it good for?
Nothing!
For it tears your families apart.

War, what is it good for?
Nothing!
For it brings us one step further away from peace.

War, what is it good for?
I say nothing!
Nothing at all!

Natalie Astle (11)
Stockland Green School

The Lost Cat

The lost cat was found in my hat
and we couldn't stop laughing
we lost her again
but were going to Spain
what are we gonna do?

This time it's not funny
we've lost a lot of money
looking here, there and everywhere
always looking, having people stare.

Where could she be?
I thought she loved me
I really miss her
it's just one big blur.

One day before we were going to go
I looked everywhere
I knew I wasn't wrong
when I found her in my case
I also knew it wouldn't be long
now we got her safe and sound
in my cuddly warm arms.

Christie-Leigh Rai (12)
Stockland Green School

SCORPIOS

I look through a book and what do I see?
Not one nice thing said about me
Scorpios are two-faced, stay away
God can't they leave us at bay?
Scorpios have a sting in their tail
Really we're not, some of us are quite frail
Scorpios are evil and are most likely to be killed
We are always being ridiculed
I will admit one thing about being a Scorpio
We are chatterboxes and that I know
A Scorpio could chat all day long
Or maybe suddenly burst into song
They say a Scorpio is forceful and calm
I know I would never put anyone at harm
To me a Scorpio is someone who is generous and kind
Never rush a Scorpio to make up their mind
Scorpios never like to see anyone hurt
A Scorpio will always help you no matter what you do
A Scorpio will always be there for you
A Scorpio is the bestest friend you could ask for
When you're with a Scorpio you could ask for nothing more
Scorpios are daydreamers and quite romantic
Scorpios are honest and very, very true
Scorpios deserve praise, just because they deserve it
Go to a Scorpio with a problem and they will chat and sit
I know myself this is true
Because all my friend's problems I have helped through
Always go to a Scorpio if you need advice
Because they will be quite nice
Scorpios are . . .

Laura Higgins (14)
Stockland Green School

Chocolate!

It's just sitting there wanting me to have it,
Its shimmering golden wrapper twinkling in the light,
Screaming, 'Buy me, buy me!'
However much I try to resist, I always give in
And this time is no exception.
I run as fast as I can into the shop
And demand that lovely moreish sweet.
I give him a handful of coins
And run out as fast as I came in.
I tear off the wrapper, put it in the bin
And take my first bite, and taste the amazing flavour
And feel the sudden rush of satisfaction, deep within me.
I take another bite and another and another,
It's so good I can't stop,
The more I eat the more I want
And I want more!
Soon the satisfaction is gone,
The chocolate sensation has finished
And I don't feel fulfilled,
So I dig into my pocket
And pull out the money.
I walk, looking for that shimmering golden wrapper
Twinkling in the light
And suddenly I find it
And I'm not going to resist at all.

Morgan Webley (14)
Stockland Green School

LIGHTHOUSE

Lighthouse light
Shining bright.
Giving warnings,
Throughout the night.

Standing tall
For all to see,
Whilst ships are out,
In the deep blue sea.

The ships sail
From nights to days.
That's why they listen
To what the lighthouse says.

The sea sways
From side to sea,
Whilst the ships are coming
Up to the tide.

Jenna Dowling (11)
Stockland Green School

SOMETIMES

Sometimes I play with my friend.
Sometimes I like to be alone.
To watch the world go by
But no one asks why?

Sometimes I laugh and be happy.
Sometimes I stare and be curious.
Sometimes I'm sad and cry
But no one asks why?

Sometimes I lie.
Sometimes I try.
Sometimes I wonder what it is like to die
But no one asks why?

Lauren Hartill (11)
Stockland Green School

Aston Villa

Aston Villa are the best
Better than all the rest
You don't need any clues
The best, De La Cruz.

Darius Vassell is the best
Better than George Best
With the speed of him
You won't see his face.

Dr Dion who's a doctor
Can make your goal tally higher
With Villa Park the best stadium
Better than Old Trafford.

Graham Taylor who's a manager
Who can work wonders
Brings joy to Villa Park
But not with blunders.

Can you beat the Villa?
Not in this millennium
With Peter Enckleman in goal
You can't beat the Villa.

Ryan McGuinness (11)
Stockland Green School

SUNDAY

It's Sunday morning
and the morning dew is just warming
the squirrels are running round and round
while hedgehogs lie on the ground
birds are sitting in the tree
while bees make honey for their tea
I am still in bed
while Dad's out getting bread
Dean is still fast asleep
while Mom's rushed off her feet
I'm up and about, I'm a lazy cow
it's time for Sunday dinner now
it's the usual Sunday routine
have a bath, make sure I'm clean
I go to my friend's
then that's how my Sunday ends.

Linzey Capewell (15)
Stockland Green School

OTTER

The sleekest swimmer you can find,
His fur is thicker than dragon hide.

When it dives it makes merely a ripple,
When it swims it is like an arrow.

Ducking and diving past debris.
It can dodge anything, even me.

It's the otter.

Mohammed Usman (11)
Stockland Green School

THE HAUNTED HOUSE

There was a house upon a hill,
In a little village called Bournville.

When it's day, it's not that scary,
But when it's night it's wise to be wary.

The house itself is long time dead,
So stay well clear or you'll lose your head.

Within these walls there are lots of stories,
With children screaming, women crying
And the men they shout, 'Beware, get out!'

That was the house up on the hill,
In the little village of Bournville.

Simmone Jones (11)
Stockland Green School

SUMMER

S ummer is the best time of the year,
Yes it is, yes it's here.
U mbrellas are not wanted now,
It's not likely to rain or snow.
M ore than likely it will shine every
Week all day long.
M y friends will just be in the park
While my brothers act out a play of Noah's ark.
E verybody will eat ice cream
While my dad sits down and watches Scream.
R unning around playing football,
After that we have to be cool.

Samuel Smith (11)
Stockland Green School

WHAT COULD IT BE?

As cold as an ice cube
As blue as the sea
As wide as the ocean
What could it be?

As red as a rose
As black as ebony
As white as snow
What could it be?

As gentle as a rabbit
As quiet as a mouse
As soft as a feather
What could it be?

As loud as an elephant
As scary as a lion
As rough as a leopard
What could it be?

Could it be a planet?
Could it be a face?
Could it be a cat?
Could it be a killer whale?

I know, do you?

Fozia Khan (11)
Stockland Green School

THE RIGHT JOB

What is the right job for me?
I want to make lots of money,
I want to be able to use my brain,
I want to feel happy,
I want to enjoy it
And I just want to be me.

Maybe I could be a scientist,
But science isn't my strong subject,
Mind you I could always learn,
But would I be happy being in a lab nearly seven days a week?
Maybe being a scientist isn't for *me*.

Maybe I could be a songwriter,
I would get a lot of money,
Mind you the songs will have to be good,
That's where using my brain comes in,
But would I enjoy writing all the time?
Nearly, but not quite the perfect job.

Maybe I could be a singer/actress,
I would make a lot of money (if I'm successful)
I would be using my brain if I write my own songs,
I would be happy to sing, dance, act
And the most important thing is I would be free to express myself
So this profession is the one for me.

I'm going to be a *star!*

Danielle Radway (14)
Stockland Green School

When I Grow Up

When I grow up I don't know what to be,
I was wondering if you could help me.
What about a singer,
To sing my favourite song?
Maybe a hairdresser,
To cut hair all day long?
An astronaut maybe,
To fly through space?
How about a plastic surgeon,
To recreate a face?
What about a poet,
To write my favourite rhyme?
I know one thing for certain
I need more time!

Gemma Stratford (14)
Stockland Green School

Spider

Climbing down its thread,
Scurrying through the bathroom,
Hiding in my bed.
He has long hairy legs,
And he makes his web from peg to peg.
He was hiding in the bin,
But when I saw him
I squashed him with a tin.

Adam Stevens (13)
Stockland Green School

Life

Troubled was this man, this man was troubled
Physically and mentally;
So he went for a walk in the park
Hoping to clear his mind of the past,
But his problem was the future.

The pleasant sounds cleared his mind
As a peaceful place he tried to find,
When he came across something that made him think.
Two paths, one led west, one east,
So he began to make his decision.

But were the paths a direction to a place
Where he can overcome his strife,
Or an important decision in the old man's life?

Reuben Reynolds (11)
Stockland Green School

Parents' Love

Parents are always there when you need a shoulder to cry on.
They're there when you need a helping hand.

They're going to be in your heart forever and ever,
Even when someone or something comes and takes them away.

You know they'll love you
In a special kind of way.

It's true,
It all comes from the heart.

Lauran Judge (11)
Stockland Green School

DAVID BECKHAM

B is for the bending balls of Beckham.
E is for the effort of England captain Beckham, number 7.
C is for the curling and catching balls of Becks.
K is for the famous David Beckham's kicking ability.
H is for his weird yet wicked haircuts.
A is for the action of the crowd when Beckham swings the ball in.
M is for the most challenging team in the Premiership, Manchester Utd.

Jordan Lindsay (11)
Stockland Green School

DARIUS VASSEL

V is for Vassel's victorious winning last minute goals.
A is for Vassel's acrobatic air skills.
S is for his superduper scoring ability.
S is for his unbelievable skills and shooting ability.
E is for extremely fast pace and control on the ball.
L is for his luscious goals and amazing talent.

Damian White (11)
Stockland Green School

BECKHAM

B end it past
E nckleman
C url it past
K ahn
H ammer it
A gainst
M cManaman.

Anthony Worledge (11)
Stockland Green School

Music Poem

I like bands like Slipknot
It is rock
But Nelly and Kelly
Is R'n'B, rap and pop.

I like to sing and dance
My friend likes to dance
Anastasia move that thing
For the lads.

I like rap
Some of it is good
Like Nelly and Kelly
Miss Dynamite as well.

I like singing and dancing
Jumping and prancing
Going mad, hit a glass, it smashed
Bad girl.

I think I'm cool at singing
I think I rule
The thing about it is that
All the boys drool.

I can dance, yes I can
Anybody would fall at my feet
Like I am a princess
And I get tanned.

I am a singing
And dancing queen
And nobody can stop me
'Cause I can be mean!

Danniella Thompson (11)
Stockland Green School